Blessed hope

The Autobiography of

JOHN F. Walvoord

with MAL COUCH

AMG Publishers
Chattanooga, TN 37421

ISBN: 0-89957-361-4

Printed in the United States of America
06 05 04 03 02 01 –S– 7 6 5 4 3 2 1

*With gratitude and thanks
for the tape transcription and typing by
Mrs. Ted Faust*

*and photography research by
Mrs. Larry Dodd*

CONTENTS

FOREWORD

It would be impossible to write the history of the evangelical church of the last half of the twentieth century without giving Dr. John Walvoord a most prominent position. For more than sixty years he has stood, without apology, for the literal interpretation of all Scripture, particularly Bible prophecy. More than any other one man he has kept the "blessed hope" of the pretribulational Rapture alive and well.

As president of Dallas Theological Seminary for thirty-four years, he guided the training of more young ministers than any other person in America. He was one seminary president who was not content with merely guiding the school and raising the money necessary to run it; Dr. Walvoord was often found teaching prophecy classes himself. He brought together one of the most qualified seminary faculties ever assembled. Names like Charles Ryrie, Dwight Pentecost, Merrill F. Unger, and Stanley Toussaint—all men committed to the literal interpretation of the Word of God and to the literal, physical return of Christ to set up His millennial kingdom.

Dr. Walvoord has been one of the most interesting prophecy teachers of the twentieth century. Even today, his name on a prophecy conference program assures a large audience. I once saw him speak to a group of fifteen hundred people, comprised largely of twenty to thirty year-olds. I wondered, as he limped up onto the platform and sat on a stool (in his late eighties it was difficult for him to stand for an hour), how this audience would receive him.

He literally captivated them. When he finished, they gave him a standing ovation. Then, during the follow-up question-and-answer period, he mesmerized those young people. When he finished, they gave him another standing ovation. And he did this sort of thing right on into his nineties. Not as often, but just as effectively.

Dr. Walvoord's writings, particularly on prophetic subjects, are interesting yet scholarly, inspiring while not being speculative, and they are accessible to the new Christian while at the same time meaningful for the Bible scholar. He is one of the most quoted pretribulational writers in the world.

Today's church owes a great debt to this man. Anyone who emphasizes the imminent coming of Christ, as has Dr. Walvoord, has helped to fire the spirit of holiness, evangelism, and missionary vision in the hearts of pastors and believers. Dr. John Walvoord has done for the present-generation church what John Nelson Darby did in the nineteenth century—he has kept the torch of prophetic expectation alive and well in the hearts of missions. Now it is the task of those thousands of us he has influenced to "keep the torch alive," for he exceeds ninety years of age and should enjoy "rest from his labors for his works do follow him."

—TIM LAHAYE
author, minister, educator

PREFACE

In the spring of 1999, I suggested to Dr. John Walvoord that he allow someone to write about his life and ministry. To my delight he gave *me* the nod, so in May 2000, we began recording conversations. Though he turned ninety that same month, some recording sessions were postponed because of his speaking engagements around the country.

Upon his return from one such engagement he shared this exciting experience with me. During the weekend he delivered a sermon on prophecy and salvation. After the message more than one hundred people made professions of faith. He has seen many people accept Christ as he shared God's Word around the world, but in all his years he had never seen that many come forward at one time.

In our time together I learned two important things about Dr. Walvoord. First, while he is an exceptional administrator and Bible teacher, in the depths of his heart he is also a soul winner. He determined many years ago that, no matter the subject he was teaching, he would always present the gospel of the saving grace of Jesus Christ. Second, his life from college on has been completely devoted to serving Christ. He has been a faithful servant who has trusted continually in the wisdom of his heavenly Master.

I am pleased to offer you highlights from the nine-decade journey of John Walvoord's life and ministry.

—Mal Couch

1

THE EARLY YEARS

I lay on the floor of the garage in excruciating pain. Six years earlier I had fought my way through a serious heart attack, followed by bypass surgery. And there I was on my back again! Slips and falls can happen fast. As I turned on the step leading down into my garage, I twisted the wrong way and fell. The intense pain told me that this wasn't good. I had been on my way to pick up my wife, Geraldine, because the car she drove was in the shop. As I lay on the garage floor, I knew I didn't want to be taken to the hospital until she got home; otherwise, it would be too great a shock for her. I called for the gardener in the backyard to get help and to get word to my wife to come home. I sent him to my brother-in-law's house down the street, where a housekeeper contacted Geraldine.

Many people have asked me, "Didn't you wonder why this happened to you?" My honest answer is no. It is my philosophy that asking why denies God's sovereignty and providence. We often will never understand the whys. That's not to say that I've not had discouragement. I have. But I've also experienced wonderful blessings in the service of the Lord.

This book is the account of my long journey in the ministry,

as told to Mal Couch. That journey of preaching and teaching
the Word of God consists of some disappointments, but it also
consists of a multitude of victories. Here is my story.

⇒ ⇐

I couldn't have been more blessed with the heritage given to
me by my parents. My mother and father were strong, stable
Christians who left me with warm memories of home and
hearth. I have many fond recollections of a home environment that was peaceful and godly, and I'm certain it served
me well over the many years of my service for Christ.

I was born on May 1, 1910, in Sheboygan, Wisconsin, a city
that lies on Lake Michigan, deep in the heart of Dutch country. I can still see in my mind's eye the two-story yellow frame
house at 1809 North Fifth Street. The cozy residence had high
windows, an attic, and a cool, damp basement where all of
the cold foods and canned goods for winter were stored.

But my arrival into this world was not a pleasant event for
my mother and father. Because Mother was ill during her preg-
nancy, the family doctor feared my birth would be traumatic
and difficult. He advised an abortion. Knowing my mother
and father, I'm sure they agonized and prayed over such a
dreadful decision. They decided, of course, to bring me into
this life, no matter what the consequences.

Family ties are important to the Dutch people, but a lot of
the history of our ancestors did not pass to us. I know that
three of my grandparents came from Holland; my grandmother on my father's side came from Germany. The initial *F*
in my name stands for Flipse, my mother's family name.
Around Sheboygan, this name was common, like Smith. Both
of my mother's parents came to this country as teenagers. As

was often the rule in immigrant homes, her parents spoke only the language of the old country. Mother recalled that she had not uttered a sentence of English before she went to public school. She was spanked the first day in class because she disobeyed the teacher. In fact, Mom couldn't understand a word the teacher had said to her.

My father's family came from Holland, and the family title was Walvoort, with a *t* at the end. *Walvoort* could describe a place having a wall and a river ford, but we're not sure. So the meaning of the name is debatable. For easier pronunciation in America, the *t* was replaced by a *d*. My father's middle name was Garrett, his mother's maiden name. My mother's family, like my paternal grandfather, came from Holland.

I know that my parents and my paternal grandparents were Christians, but I cannot speak for the entire family tree. I am certain that, for the most part, they were moral and godly people, but coming to Christ is a personal issue requiring conviction of the mind and heart. I'm certain that the family had a moral and religious bent, as did most of the Dutch immigrants. But high moral convictions do not necessarily indicate true Christian faith.

Nonetheless, my father's family positively influenced their community. A good name in those days meant a lot, and names left to and fondly remembered by posterity can also tell us a lot about a family. In Cedar Grove, where all my family ties are, there is a Walvoord street and a Walvoord monument in the cemetery, located in the center of the town. Even today, the city takes care of the property. There my father, mother, grandparents, and other relatives are laid to rest.

Cedar Grove is a farming village, about a mile from Lake Michigan. Highway 141 zigzags out of town. In a crook of the road a few miles into the country, my grandparents staked the Walvoord name to several hundred acres of farmland. Before I was born, my father had left the acreage that for so many years had belonged to the family. But the family roots go deep into the soil of this beautiful part of Wisconsin. With its green hills and slow-moving rivers, my brother, sister, and I were blessed far more than we realized to spend our childhood in such a peaceful environment.

Our parents before us enjoyed the same surroundings. Mom and Dad lived across the road from each other, about a mile outside of Cedar Grove. They had known each other from the age of four. Being only a few weeks apart in age, they had a lot in common and were childhood sweethearts. Their mutual admiration and fondness continued to grow through their teen years and on into their late twenties. Their courtship lasted about twenty-three years!

A problem hovered during all that period. My father was not a Christian, and Mother refused to marry him until he settled the matter of his salvation. As a child, Dad always went to church, and he knew all of the Bible stories from attending Sunday school. He was morally upright, but he had not exercised personal faith in Christ. Knowing my mother, I'm sure that she prayed fervently and persistently for Dad's conversion.

Meanwhile, my father went off to a teachers college, which in those days was called a "normal school." He was a good student through two years of study. That was all the training most teachers received in those days.

God sometimes takes a long time to answer prayer, because He works on a different timetable than we do. Eventually, Dad became involved in a local YMCA, which at that time was quite a soul-saving and evangelistic organization. Before long, my mother's prayers were answered. Dad made a profession of faith. Accepting Christ as Savior was not something he did simply to please my mother. His conversion was personal and intimate. His acceptance of Christ was obvious to everyone, especially to my mother. After Dad came to the Lord, Mom said *yes* to his proposal of marriage. When both were twenty-seven, John and Mary Walvoord tied the knot.

Over a ten-year period, they had three children. My older sister, Ethel, was born in 1900, and brother, Randall, came along in 1904. Because of my mother's ill health, my healthy birth in 1910 must have surprised everyone.

Throughout their lives, my mother and father were committed believers in God and His Word. Although Mother had been raised in the Dutch Reformed Church, she joined the Presbyterian church that was home to Dad. Grandfather Walvoord helped start the local assembly of that denomination, became a ruling elder, and helped the church prosper. Grandfather died in 1909, and the permanent church building was built in 1914 with funds raised by my father. In time, the church began to shift from its firm doctrinal roots. I never heard the clear message of the gospel, although from the age of twelve to fifteen I was around the church as a member and the building janitor. The buildings have now been remodeled— the gymnasium was turned into an auditorium, and the old auditorium is used as church offices. Over the years, I'm sure that many other things have changed.

My father became a public school teacher. He must have been a good one, because after he moved to Sheboygan in about 1899, he was given the job of superintendent. But in 1924, he was fired. As a public servant, he carried strong moral convictions into his job. He made known that he stood for the things of God, and almost everyone respected his moral and spiritual fortitude. But his stand brought trouble. The high school held a monthly dance, of which Dad did not approve.

He could not close it down, but he did stop the drinking of alcoholic beverages during the dances. The local beer industry was infuriated, and they put up money to get Father voted out of his superintendent's position.

Thus, at the age of fifty-one, Dad lost the job that he dearly loved. The night he came home and told the family, we were all devastated. To all of us kids, it seemed the end of the world. Dad, however, was determined to stay in the teaching profession. To do that, the family had to settle elsewhere.

God is in control of all things, even in the firing of my father. That traumatic event caused him to better himself. He took a year off from teaching to attend the University of Wisconsin, Madison, and finished his bachelor's degree with honors. Then he was called to be principal of the Stephen Bull School in Racine, where he remained through the rest of his working career.

Without question, the atmosphere at home was intellectually stimulating. My mother was a prayer warrior, and both of my folks were practical but also studious. All of his working life my father was a schoolteacher, later a superintendent of schools, and then a principal. My sister Ethel and I followed Dad's love of academics and generally brought home high grades. After finishing high school, Randall and I followed our dreams into our respective fields of interest. Randall attended the University of Wisconsin, where he received his degree in engineering.

When we moved to Racine in 1925, the Lord began to move dramatically in the lives of both my brother and me through a Presbyterian church where the gospel was presented. Later, Dad became Sunday school superintendent. The first summer after we moved, my brother attended a Sunday school class in that church taught by a lawyer. Before long, Randall accepted Christ as his personal Savior. He remained, throughout his life, a committed Christian.

In Sheboygan, I had been immersed in the church and knew all of the stories from the Bible. Besides, I had godly Christian parents who were solid spiritual role models. But coming to Christ did not happen early. I'm not sure how I avoided making a personal decision, but He was not going to let me go.

From the time I was twelve years old, I had dreamed of becoming a preacher. Although I had not made a definite decision to accept Jesus as Savior, I thought I was saved because I was good in the way I lived. Outwardly, I appeared to be a good Christian boy. I joined the church when I was nine, went through pastoral instruction classes, and memorized Scripture and the catechism. I suppose the message of salvation was presented in all of that, but I just didn't understand it. Instead, I practiced religion. I pledged in the Young People's Society that I would read my Bible and pray every day. I recall being in one class when one of the boys asked the teacher how to be saved. The teacher was an elder, but he couldn't give an answer. I never remember the gospel being fully explained, or at least made understandable. I cannot remember the pastor in Sheboygan preaching the gospel. Being very religious, some of the Dutch people in the church did not think that was necessary. They did not think that they needed Christ in a personal way. After all, they were all going to church. They thought that was enough.

An evangelist came and spoke for an entire week. He pleaded for someone to come forward, but no one did. I still remember how brokenhearted he was that no one accepted Christ. I've often wondered how he came to be invited to our church, because the way he preached was not the sort of sermon traditionally presented from our pulpit.

Our church had a succession of pastors. The pastors might have believed the gospel, but they didn't make it clear. Most of these men were probably amillennial in their views of prophecy and the return of Christ. I never recall hearing about the blessed hope, the Rapture, or the Great Tribulation. The Second Coming of the Lord was like some mysterious event, about which no one was clear.

I have never doubted the salvation of my parents. They were spiritual and never missed church. Mother taught classes and Dad was the Sunday school superintendent. We attended meetings any time the doors of the church were open, and we were an outstanding family in the congregation. Often, the pastor would come for Sunday dinner, but mother was so committed to church that she would not stay home to cook. She told the preacher when he came to the house that he would simply have to wait until the meal was ready. But somehow, with all of the church activities going on, my parents did not ask me about my personal relationship with Christ. I guess they just assumed that I was born again. But I was not.

Even though I was not a Christian until I was fifteen, early on the Lord placed people in my life that made strong impressions on me. A retired Baptist pastor in his seventies came and spoke to us one Sunday evening. He had never been very prominent in his ministry, but he seemed to be content in the place where God had placed him. For most of his life as a pastor, he had served a string of little churches in Wisconsin. Somehow his inner contentment and peace came through to me, although I really did not understand about such things at that early age. Because of him, I determined to become a preacher. I guess that was not a very good reason for wanting to serve the Lord. But God brings people and circumstances into our lives that give direction to the paths we take. What I got through that gentle Baptist preacher might be called "step one" in leading me to Christ. What the apostle Paul wrote is certainly true: "And we know that God causes all things to work together for good to those who love God, to those who are called according to His purpose" (Rom. 8:28).

"Step two" in my coming to Christ happened one day in September 1925. After we had moved to Racine, I visited a Bible class that was held in another church. Dr. William McCarrell, the pastor of the Cicero Bible Church, was preaching. I don't remember all that he said, but one statement got through to me: You can't get to heaven simply because you are doing the best you can. He said that we all are sinners and that Christ had died for us on the cross. As he told the wonderful story, he didn't give an invitation, but conviction struck me like a lightning bolt from heaven. I didn't hesitate. I immediately grabbed hold of the grace of God that Dr. McCarrell had shared with us and instantly believed that Christ's sacrifice was for me personally.

In many ways, my life wasn't different after I came to Christ. I was already living a moral life. Because my parents thought that I was a Christian all along, I don't think that they realized I had accepted Christ as Savior or how it came about. Living morally can lull a person into thinking that he or she is a Christian. But salvation comes by a definite, decisive moment when one accepts Christ as Savior. My home life was warm and comfortable, and I recall that Mother was quite outspoken about her Christian faith and her deep spiritual life. Yet the issue of my personal salvation was never discussed.

Humanly speaking, I owe much to Dr. McCarrell. He was a great soul-winner who led thousands of people to Christ because he made the gospel so plain. Although I became one of his trophies of grace, I didn't tell him until years later that I had trusted the Lord at the age of fifteen under his teaching. Dr. McCarrell went on to become a respected spiritual leader. As the years passed, he became increasingly concerned about liberal theology in the churches. To stem the tide, he became an early participant in and supporter of the Independent Fundamental Churches of America (IFCA), which was organized in 1931. I'm grateful that the Lord used Dr. McCarrell to bring me to Christ. And as it turned out, God would use Dr. McCarrell to spiritually encourage me later in life as well.

2

HOME AND SCHOOL:
THE GROWING-UP YEARS

People my age are often asked about life in the "old days." And many people have expressed an interest in knowing what it was like to grow up in the Walvoord household. As I mentioned, we had pleasant family relationships, with no deep emotional or spiritual problems. In fact, I can't recall any strife within the family, and though I was the younger brother, my older sister and brother didn't pick on me. Instead, we had a peaceful home life and order in the family. I don't believe I ever got a spanking. (I don't think I ever needed one, but that might be debatable.) I think the peaceful atmosphere in the home profoundly influenced us as children. Because our parents did not fuss at one another, we children must have gotten along well and just automatically obeyed what they said. Although our spiritual conversations were not deep, Dad led us in daily devotions, and I can still picture Mom on her knees by the bed each evening, praying for all of us kids.

Because she was raised in a strict Dutch Reformed church, my mother must have considered it a religious duty and a labor of love to care for her family. As the chill of fall began to fill the air, she would put up hundreds of jars of cherries,

applesauce, and rhubarb. As kids, our job was to help Mom
pack the cellar with the food that she canned for the extreme
Wisconsin winters.

And what cold and icy winters we had! Only one who has
lived near the Great Lakes can appreciate that harsh climate.
When we lived in Sheboygan, my father took on the task of
being the church janitor, a job he held for many years without any compensation. In the early morning on icy winter
Sundays, Dad went to the church and lit the hot-air coke furnaces. Later, my brother took on the task, but by then the
congregation had decided that the job of janitor was no small
task and paid him fifteen dollars a month. I don't think Dad
asked for any back pay. Then, when my brother went off to
college and I was twelve, I took his place. The church building
had two huge furnaces, which consumed at least a ton of fuel
on cold Sundays. Those giant stoves had to heat a gymnasium, Sunday school rooms, and an auditorium. During extremely cold weather, it took all day Saturday to get the
buildings heated. Lighting the furnaces and keeping them
going was quite an undertaking for a youngster like me.

Besides taking care of the church furnaces, I was responsible for the water pipes. Every Sunday evening and on Thursday evenings following the prayer services and Boy Scout
meetings, the water had to be turned off, drained from the
pipes, and later turned back on. If we did not turn off the
water, the pipes would freeze. Keeping up with all of this was
not easy for a young boy. Looking back on it now, I'm not
sure that I did a good job, but those duties helped instill a
sense of responsibility in me at an early age.

I have many fond memories and humorous recollections
of my grade school years. I attended a brick school building
only a block from our house. My second grade teacher was a

kind person, but my third grade teacher was a stern, unmarried woman who rarely smiled. One day our school principal suddenly died, and my teacher came into the classroom with a sad face. She told us the funeral would be the next day and there would be no classes. All of us were so grateful to miss a day of school that we cheered!

Despite this instance of inappropriate behavior, I wasn't really a bad boy in school. I don't remember being paddled. In fact, I was never even sent to the principal's office for any misconduct. One of my teachers, though, was a terrible disciplinarian, and she just could not manage her class. One of the boys was so out of control that this teacher threatened to throw him out of the second floor window. In a smart-mannered way he answered back, "Go ahead!" I've wondered from time to time what he was like when he grew up.

After school and on weekends, Wisconsin winters didn't bother us as kids. We could ski down hills near Lake Michigan after snowstorms. I recall one very bad blizzard. In those days, the schools were not closed because of severe weather, and I skied to the high school, which was about a mile and a half away. Out of a high school student body of one thousand, only fifty of us got to class that day.

We did have a car. Sometime before the 1920s, Dad purchased a Willys Knight automobile. When Randall became old enough to drive, he tore around so fast that the valves burned out every one thousand miles. Father got a newer model Willys without valves. Dad loved the Willys Knight touring car and had one until the day he died in 1932. My brother taught me to drive when I turned fourteen. Learning to drive at that age was not unusual. I imagine, though, that I was a threat to everything and everybody on the road!

When we moved to Racine in 1925, I recall a lot of warm,

sunny summers, during which I did absolutely nothing but loaf. Then I turned fifteen and decided to go out for high school football. The coach was really tough and put us all through a rigorous practice program. I became terribly stiff and sore from the demanding workouts. But some additional exercises seemed to give me an edge. I had to walk a mile, for instance, to the town library to borrow books for my school assignments. That was pure torture because I was so sore from football workouts. When I got to the library and saw the twenty steps leading up to the door, I thought I'd never make it into the building. But I discovered that if I walked backward up the steps, I could make it to the entrance. There must be a lesson in this somewhere: If things don't go well, turn them around, and try another way. Maybe I learned from that experience to be persistent and not become easily discouraged.

As I got further along in high school, I gained some status as an athlete. As a teenager, I shot up to six feet, four and one-half inches tall. I played football and basketball, heaved the shot put, and threw the discus. Although I lettered in sports and must have been a big man on campus, I'm not sure how good an athlete I really was. Our entire football team might not have been that outstanding, since we won only half our games. When I graduated from high school in 1928, I received the American Legion Gold Medal for the best athlete in my January graduating class of one hundred students. But there were no other athletes in my graduating class! I guess I won the consolation prize.

Although I might not have been the best athlete in the world, participating in competitive sports played a part in developing the perseverance and patience that I later had in the ministry. As with sports, serving the Lord can sometimes be frustrating. At times, one wants to toss in the towel. But, as in football, you just cannot stop and walk off the field when the score is against you. Under God's providence, every experience in life, every bump and bruise, plays a role in our spiritual development. Those trials give us the resolve to stay the course when disappointments come.

I succeeded fairly well in my studies. I was a member of the National Honor Society, held a scholastic score of ninety, and graduated with honors. One course in particular helped in the years that followed. Although our high school Latin course was not that impressive, I took the subject anyway, thinking that it would help me understand grammar and learn other languages later on. The teacher didn't press us very hard, but taking Latin helped sharpen my communication and language skills in general. It helped me prepare for college Latin and for my later studies of Hebrew and Greek.

Looking back upon my growing-up years, I have no doubt about the importance of the spiritual values and sense of industry that my mother modeled. But I've also often thanked the Lord for the role my father played in forming and directing my later years as an adult. I am grateful for the way my father lived, because I know that his struggles and successes, both as a schoolteacher and as a Christian, greatly influenced me. Dad had the tenacity and strength to keep going when a situation looked bleak. He returned to school so that he could provide for his family. Spiritually, he was consistent and steady. Although my father was not as expressive about his faith as was my mother, he lived out his Christian walk as a ruling elder and teacher in his church. As loyal servants of Jesus, both of my parents were shining examples to me as well as to everyone who knew them.

3

THE COLLEGE YEARS

College was the next thing to do. I was, after all, planning to go into the ministry. It also seemed a natural choice. As a schoolteacher, I'm sure my father influenced me. But God in other ways caused me to desire the best preparation I could get to serve Him. It all seemed to fall into place after we moved to Racine.

The Union Tabernacle in Racine, which later became Racine Bible Church, invited visiting Bible teachers to come on Sundays and sometimes during the week. I attended many of those sessions. Although I did not realize it then, I was exposed to some of the greatest Bible teachers living at that time. I sat spellbound as I heard for the first time someone teach on Bible prophecy. At first I didn't understand the significance of what he taught, but something in the message intrigued me. Glued to my seat, I listened to Arno C. Gaebelein describe the predicted confederation of the ten nations or, as some called it, the coming United States of Europe. I couldn't grasp what he said, but his teaching ability was not to blame. The problem was in my own biblical training. To that point, I had never been exposed to anyone who taught the full counsel of God and explained Bible prophecy. Realizing that the promises of the messianic kingdom were to be taken literally, Gaebelein was excited about the restoration of national Israel. As he explained the Old Testament prophecies, a door opened for me, and parts of the Bible were revealed to me that I had never seen before.

I was also privileged to hear H. A. Ironside, a practical, down-to-earth teacher of the Word. My parents invited him for dinner at our home, and I spoke to him later at his church. Years later he came to Dallas, Texas to see his son Ed, who helped start the Southern Bible Training School. For many years when Dr. Ironside was in Dallas, he would lecture at the seminary for many hours each week. Although he was self-taught, he had a way of making the Scriptures easy to understand. He became a nationally known dispensationalist teacher and traveled across the country making the Bible alive to large audiences. From 1930 to 1948, he was pastor of Moody Memorial Church in Chicago. Over the years, I became closely acquainted with him and found him to be a beloved and godly servant of Christ.

During those early days in Racine, another great privilege was to meet Dr. Lewis Sperry Chafer, who in 1924 founded the Evangelical Theological College, which was to become Dallas Theological Seminary. Some people thought that his only talent lay in song leading, but he had been teaching the Bible for a number of years. Unquestionably, he knew the Scriptures well. I had dinner with Dr. Chafer when he came to speak in Racine. I was only sixteen at the time and going with a girl of one of the leading lay members in the church. The girl's family invited me to join them. I probably spent more time listening to someone else at the table than to Dr. Chafer.

Although I was fascinated with the teachings of prophecy,

hearing these men did not suddenly bring on a strong awakening to the subject. That would come years later in seminary as I began to see the full plan of Scripture. But these men certainly introduced me to truths in God's Word that I had never seen before. Their spiritual influence probably helped steer me to Wheaton College after high school.

Many from my high school crowd were heading off to institutions of higher learning. One option for me was Carroll College, a Presbyterian school in Waukesha, Wisconsin. My sister Ethel graduated from Carroll, and my brother attended for two years. Randall then transferred to the University of Wisconsin, where he finished his degree in engineering. Although Carroll College was supposedly religious, I don't think it had a clear statement of faith and doctrine. My brother evidently did not hear the gospel while he was attending that school. Only later did he invite Christ into his life.

In January 1928, I decided to attend Wheaton, located in Wheaton, Illinois. At that time, the school had a strong and godly president in Dr. James Oliver Buswell. In fact, I had heard him speak before at the Union Tabernacle in Racine. Wheaton was gaining notice because of its strong faculty, trained alumni, and outstanding students, among them evangelist Percy Crawford. Crawford was ten years older than most of his classmates. During evangelism week that first January at Wheaton, he was the keynote speaker for five days. Over and over, he pleaded with the students to come to Christ. But he also urged all of us to surrender our lives to the Lord for full-time service. I'd never taken that step publicly, and I recall how challenged I was by what he said. I went forward and knelt at the altar, really meaning business with the Lord; I was going to commit my life totally to Him.

To please the Lord, I decided to do the hardest thing I could think of: I was ready to leave America and be a missionary to China. I might have been influenced by my mother, who had expressed her own desire to serve in foreign missions but never made it. It wasn't long, however, before I became confused. A missionary from China spoke at Wheaton. He said that everyone should go to China unless the Lord blocked the way. Then a missionary came from Africa and said that everyone should go to Africa unless the Lord blocked the way.

I thought, "Wait a minute! Is this the way the Lord really calls us into His service?" This humanly inspired dogmatism left uncertainty about my call to the mission field. I thought about the problem for months and was in a spiritual quandary, but I never lost a concern for missions itself. God seemed to use all that to point me in another direction.

When I first went to Wheaton, I determined to major in Greek in preparation for studying a foreign language I would use in missionary service. Because the college required that every student take something from the science department, I minored in physics. Over the years, the Greek helped me to better understand the Bible. When a student majored in Greek, the school also required him to take Latin. In my case, this was *more* Latin after my high school study. Miss Harriet Blaine, my Latin teacher at Wheaton, was a tyrant in language who cracked the whip over the heads of the eight students in her class. I barely passed each year because I had very competitive and intelligent classmates. In fact, two classmates went on to earn doctorates in Latin. Although I was under a lot of pressure, perseverance and tenacity came to my rescue again, and I would not give up Latin.

At Wheaton, I wanted to go out for football, but the rumors were that football team players would not have the study time to pass the tough Greek studies. And, lo and behold, my first Greek teacher was Miss Blaine. I think she was out to keep the rumors alive because she always unmercifully slashed the sentence exercises I put on the blackboard. I think that she did her best to flunk me, but I refused to give up. One time she gave me a score of sixty on a paper. I pointed out to her that I thought she'd made a mistake. She raised the grade to a ninety, probably with great reluctance!

One night, I took a girl to a school musical. This girl was also a Greek student, but she was having a lot of problems with the subject. Miss Blaine ran into us as we walked to the program. We were in for trouble because she expected us to be in our rooms preparing our assignments for the next day. I got up at four A.M. and crammed into my brain all of the Greek I could. Sure enough, when it came time to recite sentences, Miss Blaine immediately called on the girl I had taken to the musical. She sheepishly answered, "Not prepared." I knew what was coming when Miss Blaine turned to me. Nervously stuttering, I seemed to be totally dumbstruck. She finally cut me off and gave me a zero for the day. Although I ended the semester with an average of 87.5, she cut the grade down to an eighty-five because her grading system rounded to fives, such as 80, 85, or 90. At the time I thought that Miss Blaine was awfully tough on us poor students, but she forced us to be diligent and earnest about our academics.

Later, I was blessed in classical Greek with Dr. George H. Smith. Dr. Smith was in his eighties, and he loved to watch the Wheaton football team play! He inspired me to work harder, and I held an *A* average all the way through his courses. As I came to my senior year, the school required 240 grade points for graduation with honors. I was coming up short several points, so I went to Dr. Smith and another teacher and asked if I could do extra assignments to bring up my grades.

They both agreed to the additional work, and I ended up with exactly what I needed—240 grade points. Although I barely squeaked by, I did earn honors while involved in sports and in various Christian organizations on campus.

Although my grades at Wheaton were okay overall, I wonder how I pulled it off. Besides Christian ministry, I was involved in all kinds of activities. After achieving a grade point average of ninety, for example, I was elected to Pi Kappa Delta, the honorary forensic society. I was also in the debating society, which held national and regional competitions in alternate years in debate and oratory. We debated such issues as the Compulsory Unemployment Insurance program, today known as Social Security. By unanimous decision of the judges, our men's team won eight of the ten debates, whichever side of the question we argued.

I also joined the men's intercollegiate debate team. This group of six students was considered the most successful debate team in Wheaton's history. We participated in fifty competitions against twenty-six colleges and universities over two years without losing a debate.

Maybe I did all that debating because I simply enjoyed a good argument. On several occasions, I worked out some of the debate strategies. No doubt this debating sharpened my thinking processes for future theological battles.

I was pretty good in football, although some people might argue that point. I played tackle for three years on the Wheaton team, which was nicknamed the "Orange and Blue." The yearbook says that I was "A giant in mold" (whatever that means). But it added that I was a hard-hitting, fast-charging lineman. (That sounds better!) Our team had its on-and-off years, losing to the mighty DeKalb Teachers College. The yearbook says that they rode into town with a bewildering, powerful attack and "repeatedly marched down the field in spite of the plucky battle put up by the Wheaton men."

I also ran track and threw the discus and was good enough each year to earn my letter. The yearbook says that the Lake Forest College squad easily defeated Wheaton in the field competitions and implied that we were so weak that we lacked material to take even second or third in the competition. I guess that was a kind way of referring to me, too. Our entire squad apparently lacked great athletic prowess.

To keep in shape for sports, I worked hard during the summers. One summer I dug ditches for the electric company where my brother had some influence because he was employed as an engineer. I worked six days a week at fifty cents an hour, slaving away with a team of men in ninety-degree heat that was intensified by the humidity coming off Lake Michigan. During another summer, I laid streetcar tracks. I went home covered with dirt and grime, and had to take a shower every day. But hard labor didn't hurt any of the students who had to work "by the sweat of their brow" to earn money for school. We all survived, and the manual labor taught us to work hard. Ministerial students should toughen up with exercise. Physical labor plays a part in preparing men for spiritual struggles with the souls of people.

Despite earning about two hundred dollars in summer jobs, paying the one thousand dollars a year to attend Wheaton was a struggle. I worked for a short time waiting dinner tables at school, but my parents still paid about eight hundred dollars a year. I was grateful. At the time Dad made only three thousand dollars a year as a school principal, so eight hundred dollars represented a little over twenty-five percent of his yearly salary! But he was always there for his children so that we could all attend college.

Besides working at manual labor during the summers, in 1929 I started doing missionary vacation Bible school in Nebraska. I sacrificed seventy-five dollars for a 1926 Dodge. Although that automobile took me over one thousand miles of dirt roads from Illinois to western Nebraska, it had a big problem: I could drive only about twenty-five miles an hour. If I sped up to thirty, the car nearly fell apart from vibration. If I cranked the speed up to forty, the radiator cap blew off and great clouds of steam billowed out from under the hood. After puttering along at twenty-five miles per hour all day, I couldn't wait to find motel rooms for the night.

One summer I stayed in Rushville, Nebraska, and each day drove the twenty miles over to Gordon, a prairie town of two thousand. We gathered children from several area churches and spent two weeks teaching the Bible. Although the grade school was closed for the summer, the town fathers opened it so we could teach the 225 kids. Pastors were delighted to have someone teach the Bible classes for them. It was an amazing experience, and many youngsters came to Christ. Each class started with fifteen minutes of music, followed by Scripture study. We also told missionary stories and allowed time for recess on the playground. Children earned points for attending, memorizing verses, and bringing new visitors. I wrote the study curriculum and even directed a play for the older children. Using sheets for costumes, the kids acted out Noah and the ark and events from the books of Esther and Ruth. The kids loved it, and I'm certain that those children from that small, rural town never forgot those days. They probably told their grandchildren about the traveling Bible teachers who brought something that was both entertaining and spiritual. Our prayers were always for the salvation of the children and for their growth in the Lord.

It seemed somehow easier in those days to reach children for Christ. There was no television, and people had very little money for travel or to attend the theater. The parents encouraged their children to get out of the house and come to our classes. Often, I drove around the community and picked up the youngsters in my car. Altogether, I conducted fifty of these two-week Bible schools. That's grassroots ministry and evangelism, and there's no training like it for preparing to minister in other areas. In spite of disappointments, the efforts were rewarding. It's humbling, too, for someone who wants to be a servant of Christ to stoop down and spend time with children. God honors those who are faithful in such a task by giving them more responsibility in future service.

My sister had married Edward C. Raue, a Presbyterian minister who served a church in Scottsbluff, Nebraska. He had some influence with the denomination's regional office, and later, during some of those summers, he got me appointed as the Sunday school missionary for the area, with a salary of one hundred dollars per month. Although some of the local churches were closed during the heat of the summer, I sometimes preached around the countryside in the churches that were open. One summer, Edward gave me a chance to preach in his church in Scottsbluff. I don't think he knew what he was getting the congregation into. I came up with a strange subject—"A Child's God!" I think the message lasted only about thirteen minutes. I followed up on other Sundays with two other messages: "A Young Person's God" and then "An Adult's God." I don't remember the people swarming around me afterward with congratulations on my great oratory. One woman, however, came up and said, "If you don't preach any longer than you did today, I'll be back next Sunday." What torture some churches endure with ministers who are wet behind the ears!

On one occasion, I journeyed into South Dakota to hold vacation Bible school for 125 children, some of whom had to ride more than five miles on horseback to attend the meetings. We met in a consolidated school house miles from any town. The people in those areas were wide open to the gospel and Bible instruction. Not all of them were born again, but no one opposed the Word of God. Basically, they were good farm people.

I stayed several summers in Rushville, Nebraska, with Mr. and Mrs. Preble. He was an older man whose first wife had died, and his second wife, who was a nurse, was younger than he. She was a big woman, and he was small and thin. It was quite interesting to see them together, and they were extremely kind to me.

Those farmhouse rooms were awfully hot during the summer nights. I sent off for a four-dollar electric fan from Sears and Roebuck. The fan helped, except when I had to close the bedroom windows because of the dust storms.

Although I preached a little at my brother-in-law's church in Scottsbluff, you could say I really cut my preaching teeth in Rushville. Preaching was difficult for me at first, so I wrote out all my messages in full. I spent Saturday afternoon delivering those sermons out loud to the empty pews in the church. On Sunday, forty or fifty people sat on hard pews and endured what I had to say. A wise physician tried to encourage me after my messages. He said, "There's always room at the top." I think he meant that I was then on the bottom and could only go one way! I'm sure he would have been surprised to find out that I later became the president of a seminary.

By the time I was an upperclassman at Wheaton, I was blessed with a lot of ministry experience both at school and during the summers. In my junior year, I became president of the student volunteer organization, which was mainly involved with missions. In my senior year, I was president of Christian Endeavor and, with a student staff of six, I was responsible for scheduling outside speakers. Of a student body of five hundred, we had more than two hundred students attend our meetings on Sunday nights. Sometimes we divided into small groups for spiritual discussions. The students really enjoyed these informal sessions.

I'm often asked, "What were the burning issues among Christian college students in those days?" A continuing topic of discussion was fundamentalism versus liberalism. In one sense, things were kind of cut and dried. If you were liberal, you didn't read your Bible; if you were a fundamentalist, you did. Although Wheaton College was premillennial in teaching at that time, eschatology didn't figure much in conversations. Wheaton was very biblical, and in the spring and summer special studies were held on the spiritual life and the doctrine of personal salvation. Also, prayer meetings were held in the morning and there were revivals on campus each semester. Morning prayer meetings at the start of the academic year swelled to more than one hundred. But human nature set in, and the attendance soon was down to about thirty. My spiritual hunger was growing, and I was always at these sessions.

My college roommate, Wilton Nelson, and I helped each other spiritually. For three years, I roomed with Wilton, who was a good student and an outstanding young man who greatly loved the Lord and served Him throughout his life. He went on to earn his doctorate at Princeton. He became the director of the Latin American Missions Seminary in Guatemala City, Guatemala. At that time, Central America was a very backward area. Poverty crippled the population, and disease ravaged adults and children. Ignorance and religious darkness kept the masses in spiritual bondage. It was not a pleasant environment in which to minister. I always admired Wilton for his dedication to serve in that part of the world. With his training, he could have chosen a more comfortable job, but his missionary calling was both sacrificial and genuine.

My college years were also formative years in which the Lord prepared me. He opened my eyes to many things and set a course that would present many personal challenges. But the next big step would come as I attended seminary.

4

THE SEMINARY STUDENT YEARS

As I neared completion at Wheaton, I began thinking seriously about seminary. But which one? Although we students knew about the fundamentalist/modernist controversy, we weren't fully aware of the doctrinal ramifications. To help in making my decision, I examined the catalogs of several schools. I studied the thin Dallas Theological Seminary catalog and wasn't impressed. The school was barely off the ground and had only sixty students and three professors. I was attracted to the catalog of Princeton Seminary, the pride of the Presbyterian church. Many of my friends were planning to attend this prestigious institution. But every time I prayed about where to go, I kept coming back to Dallas.

To get some help, I went to the office of Wheaton's president, Dr. James Oliver Buswell, who had just received an honorary degree from Dallas Seminary. He sat in his big chair and listened patiently to my problem. When I finished, he said that he thought I would receive a great education if I went to Dallas. That settled it. I determined to begin in the fall of 1931 after graduation from Wheaton in June. One other great Bible teacher also helped me to decide on Dallas. Dr. B. B. Sutcliffe had a big church and a Bible institute in Portland, Oregon, but he was also a visiting teacher at Dallas. When he came to Wheaton to speak at our Christian Endeavor meetings, I was able to talk to him as well. He spoke highly of Dallas, and wrote a letter of recommendation for me, urging them to accept me as a student.

God had surely placed circumstances and people in my path, leading me to where He wanted me. I was on the way to Dallas, Texas. Wheaton graduates comprised twenty-five percent of my class at Dallas; many already were personal friends. I had no way of knowing at that time the awesome direction that my life would take.

Humanly speaking, none of us at Dallas at that time fully realized the debt of gratitude we owed to Dr. Lewis Sperry Chafer. Although he was a good Bible teacher, his legacy lies in his vision for starting Dallas Seminary.

In 1871, Lewis Chafer was born the second of three children to Thomas and Lomira Chafer in Rock Creek, Ohio. His father was a graduate of Auburn Theological Seminary, a Presbyterian/Congregational institution in New York state. Chafer's father, a godly pastor who served a small congregation in Rock Creek, fought a losing war with the scourge of that day—tuberculosis. He tried to be a devoted and caring father and preacher, but the disease brought a constant strain on the family. In 1882, he lost the battle, and the sound of laughter and music died in that joyful Christian home. But Lewis's mother, Lomira, was a strong, spiritual woman who devised a plan to put the family back on course.

Lomira moved the family to Oberlin, Ohio, where the children could attend the Conservatory of Music of Oberlin College. Chafer studied there for three semesters from 1889 to 1891. Although no indications exist that he took Bible courses at Oberlin, he later studied theology informally under some of the best premillennial and dispensational teachers in America. In 1889, he became interim pastor of the First Presbyterian Church of Lewiston, New York, although that same year he also became the assistant pastor of the First Congregational Church of Buffalo. In 1890, he was ordained as a Congregational minister, and in 1896, he married Ella Lorraine Case, who would join him at the church as organist.

Although Chafer had a pastor's heart, he also longed to win people to Christ. He began traveling to Bible conferences and evangelistic meetings where he directed the choir programs. His wife also became part of the evangelism teams as organist. During the years that followed, he sat under the teaching ministry of such men of God as G. Campbell Morgan, F. B. Meyer, A. C. Gaebelein, James M. Gray, W. H. Griffith Thomas, and C. I. Scofield. Chafer emerged as a quiet, energetic leader of the growing dispensational movement among evangelicals.

Chafer joined the staff of New York School of the Bible, an agency that distributed Scofield's increasingly popular Bible correspondence course, on which his Bible notes were based. In 1913, Chafer assisted Scofield in founding Philadelphia School of the Bible. In the 1880s, Scofield had been pastor at a Congregational church in Dallas, Texas, but he later moved on to other ministries. Although Scofield was not pastor of the Dallas congregation when he died on July 24, 1921, the church wanted to continue his strong doctrinal leadership and keep the spiritual legacy going. With his health declining from so much traveling, Chafer needed to settle down. He moved to Dallas in 1922 to become the pastor of Scofield's old church. But, as important as was the church work, other plans were brewing in Chafer's mind.

As Chafer and other great Bible teachers moved about the

country, they saw the need for a new seminary. The reason was obvious: liberalism was eroding the theological foundations at schools and churches. In the first quarter of the twentieth century, many of the historically orthodox mainline denominational seminaries, such as Princeton, were turning away from teaching the Bible. Although the Presbyterian denomination tolerated pastors who were dispensational, a growing number of seminary professors sneered at premillennial and dispensational teaching. Besides being Reformed in their leanings, many schools had been increasingly influenced by the biblical liberalism coming from England and especially Germany for a century. I was not unaware of these growing concerns, but neither was I then perceptive enough to see what was on the horizon. The great theological rift was not far away.

In fact, Princeton Seminary was undergoing painful theological turmoil during the 1920s. J. Gresham Machen and some of the conservative professors and board members fought a rear guard action to try to stop the liberal takeover of the school. Machen and other conservatives were rebuffed at the seminary and at the General Assembly of the northern Presbyterian Church in the United States of America (PCUSA). Several Princeton professors resigned and moved to form Westminster Theological Seminary on September 25, 1929. Many other fine seminaries were also moving to the left in their teaching. Presbyterian church historian David B. Calhoun has spent much of his life studying the old Princeton theology and assessing the complex reasons why Princeton moved from its evangelical position (David B. Calhoun, *Princeton Seminary*, vol. 2 [Carlisle, Pa.: Banner of Truth, 1996, p. 398).

The problems began in the early 1800s with a drift toward classic nineteenth century liberalism among leaders of the denomination. By the turn of the twentieth century, mainline Presbyterians of the PCUSA had turned away from the solid fidelity to Scripture in the Old Princeton message. They elected to maintain institutional unity at the expense of doctrinal integrity. As would later happen in the Southern PCUSA, the northern church opened the door to syncretism with the culture. It became increasingly difficult for the church to sustain its Christian witness to the next generations. This is a sobering lesson all ministers of the Word of God must heed.

An important point must be made here. As prolific as liberalism and modernism were becoming, Chafer did not found Dallas as a protest against these trends. He began the school to counter the lack of Bible teaching in seminaries and churches. He wanted the seminary to teach the Word of God, much as many of the Bible institutes were doing. His goal also was to train and prepare men as faculty for those schools. Over the years, Dallas has accomplished this objective. Dallas Seminary graduates have staffed many institutions.

In early 1923, Chafer held a Bible conference in the big, downtown Dallas First Presbyterian Church, one of the largest churches of the denomination in the South. He shared his dream of starting a Bible-centered seminary with Dr. William Anderson, who at the time was an outstanding pastor and leader among Presbyterians. Anderson had the respect of Presbyterians and leaders of other denominations in the area. He quickly called a meeting, to which about sixty businessmen came. After much prayer, they decided to start the Evangelical Theological College (later Dallas Theological Seminary). They appointed a fifteen-member board of trustees, mainly from First Presbyterian Church and Scofield Memorial Church, with Chafer's brother Rollin acting as the first registrar and admissions officer.

About a half a mile from downtown Dallas and not too far

from the First Presbyterian Church, two wooden, two-story apartment buildings were rented. These became the first classrooms and offices. In 1928, an Oklahoma oilman named Adam Davidson pledged one hundred thousand dollars for building on the school's first piece of property on Swiss Avenue. Davidson lived by feast or famine, as the petroleum business went up and down. But he finally came through with this large amount, and Davidson Hall was constructed. During the Depression, Davidson lost most of his money, but I'm sure he never regretted making the sacrifice that helped launch the school's building program. In faraway Philadelphia, God touched Daniel Miner Stearns. A successful and talented Episcopalian Bible teacher, he held a series of Bible studies in the Philadelphia area. Because he earnestly believed in what was happening so quickly at the seminary, he took up offerings in his classes and donated the funds for a second building, the Reverend Daniel Miner Stearns Hall, which was constructed in 1927 and 1928. The supporter's son, Miner Stearns, attended DTS and received his Th.B. and Th.M. in 1929 and his Th.D. in 1942.

In those early days, crises arose that, from the human perspective, could have closed the seminary. During 1928 and 1929, the board thought that even though new buildings had been built, financially the school just couldn't go on. In the spring of 1929, about the time of commencement, the seminary needed ten thousand dollars to remain open. If that amount didn't come in, the plan was to make an announcement at the graduation ceremonies that this was the end of the school. Unknown to Dr. Chafer and others, an Illinois banker, an uncle of Dr. Charles Ryrie, had been postponing for months sending a ten thousand dollar gift to the school. He finally dropped the check in the mail. Chafer had set the deadline for this need to be met on the morning the day before commencement. Five minutes before the 9:00 A.M. deadline, as he and Dr. Ironside were discussing their financial problem in his office, a secretary brought in the envelope with the funds. The seminary never again had a crisis quite like that.

Clearly, the hand of God was in these gifts that came along for the seminary so quickly in the school's early years. The Depression that would fall upon the nation in October 1929 was just over the horizon. With so many businesses failing during those dark economic times, carrying out expansions of the buildings should have been impossible. Unquestionably, the Lord was blessing the establishment of the school. But it's interesting to note *how* He brought about this support.

Years before the establishment of DTS, the seeds were being planted by godly premillennial and dispensational Bible teachers who moved around the country teaching at conferences and in churches. People were being blessed by the thousands in their understanding of the Word of God.

When Dallas Seminary was established as one of the first premillennial schools, the rallying cry for support could be heard in far-off places. In the beginning, many Presbyterians supported Dallas's founding. Some of them questioned premillennialism but accepted dispensationalism. At least most tolerated these teachings. The war against the seminary would heat up as Southern Presbyterians followed the northern church into liberalism and the attack on fundamentalism.

Meanwhile, in the fall of 1931, I was ready to begin my graduate theological education at Dallas. By that time, the school had the two new main buildings. When Chafer started the school, it had only a few resident faculty and staff members, although many godly and respected guest lecturers came and taught special courses. Even the well-respected Englishman William Henry Griffith Thomas had accepted an invitation to lecture at the school before he died suddenly in 1924. The seminary was later bequeathed the library from his estate.

When I arrived on campus with twenty-five others, the school had jumped from the sixty students mentioned in DTS's catalog to around eighty. At the time, the school was granting a three-year Bachelor of Theology (Th.B.) degree and, by adding a certain number of electives to that program, the Master of Theology (Th.M.) degree. In 1936, the school dropped the Th.B. and simply focused on continuing the stronger Th.M. and Doctor of Theology (Th.D.) degrees.

The seminary students were indeed blessed to study under knowledgeable and dedicated professors. One teacher, who was pastor for a Presbyterian church just outside of Dallas, drove every day or so to the school for classes. One of my outstanding professors was Everett F. Harrison, who had been a missionary in Hunan Province, China. He held two bachelor degrees, one from Princeton University and one from Princeton Seminary. He also had an M.A. and a Ph.D. from the University of Pennsylvania. He later received his Th.D. from Dallas. Harrison was well qualified to teach New Testament Greek, but because the school already had a Greek teacher, he taught Hebrew his first year.

Dallas Seminary was a dispensational school, but it would be misleading to say that it was built upon *The Scofield Reference Bible,* which was so popular at that time. Rather, the influence of the *Scofield Bible,* with its plain dispensational teaching, was pervasive throughout the entire world of fundamentalism. Following Scofield's death, his Bible version became even more popular. Throughout the 1920s, and even later, the *Scofield Bible* was, in fact, the standard study Bible for orthodox fundamentalism.

The popularity of the *Scofield Bible* is owed, in part, to Bible institutes of higher learning and to the Bible conference movement. Both the institutes and the conferences really caught on after World War I. Their speakers recommended that Christians purchase *The Scofield Reference Bible*. Thus dispensationalism came to be considered by many as part of fundamentalism.

In fact, but for the publication of the *Scofield Bible,* Oxford Press in England would have gone bankrupt. Oxford Press was grateful for the worldwide response. Scofield's work helped people understand for the first time the plan of God that is revealed from Genesis to Revelation, and it helped people understand the Church Age and how prophecy unfolds.

DTS students, too, learned more deeply of all theological matters, from the finest experts of that time. Texas is hot in late spring and early fall. Electric fans worked hard to keep the students cool and awake. But the good teachers and interesting courses also helped. For the first time, the Bible really started coming alive for me; I knew for certain that I was in the right place.

The students were motivated, too, by their love and respect for Dr. Chafer. Physically small in stature, Dr. Chafer was extremely gentle and caring toward the students. But when he taught systematic theology, he started us out with bibliology, but he didn't use a textbook. We all had to scribble as hard as we could to keep up. Finally, some enterprising student took down his notes and began to sell them. That bit of business thinking forced Chafer himself to publish the notes in mimeographed form. I guess he liked and trusted me because I got the job of writing them up, editing the material, and sorting the pages. I didn't realize it at the time, but Dr. Chafer would begin to lean more on me.

During the first few summer breaks at DTS, I continued missionary work in Nebraska. But during the school year I preached every Sunday. I finally got a regular Sunday teaching assignment with a little group of Christians meeting in a schoolhouse in a small community called Sublet, five miles south of the town of Arlington. After preaching there in the morning I sometimes drove over to Pantego and preached there at night. On occasion my future brother-in-law, Ellwood Evans, went with me. We'd stay after the evening service and hold Bible instruction. I sometimes taught one course and Ellwood would teach another course. This was during the worst part of the Depression, and the church didn't pay anything. I don't know how I made it financially, since I had the expense of driving my own car to these meetings. God was good and so were the people. Many of them were so poor they didn't even own cars. To compensate, each Sunday they stuffed us with homemade rolls and fried chicken.

Out of appreciation or guilt, those dear folks thought that they should do something to show their love before I left for the summer break. One man who had a Ford Model T went around and collected eggs. Because I was single, he knew that I couldn't do anything with them, so he sold them to the Leonard Brothers department store for the wholesale price of nine cents a dozen. During the last Sunday evening meeting, he made a speech and proudly presented me with the egg money of $3.06. That was the largest gift I had received during the year and a half that I'd been there, and it was a lot of money for those hard economic times. I don't know how any of us made it through the Depression years, but God is gracious, and we had all that we needed to survive.

Regardless of (or perhaps because of) the difficult economic times, the people who were involved with the seminary took the training of young men for the ministry as serious business. They wanted the men studying on campus to look like well-respected and intelligent future pastors. Meals were very formal and were considered a social occasion. Except during extremely hot weather, we were required to wear coats and ties to the dining hall. A stern-looking little lady stood at the door of the dining hall and inspected each student. She ensured that we had on shoes, tie, and coat. The ministry was to be taken as a godly profession, and would-be preachers had to dress the part.

The school charged us one dollar a day for meals. The food wasn't fancy, but it was good. Because the trustees met on campus each Thursday, we had steak on those days. I guess the seminary was putting on the Ritz, but none of us students complained!

Many of the students were still boys at heart—including me. We often had water fights in the dorm, and a flood sometimes poured down the stairs. When they put in carpet, the water fights and accompanying fun ended. One time in Stearns Hall, the guys were emptying a fellow's room as a prank. As they carried his furniture down to the first floor, Dr. Chafer walked in. For certain, the men didn't want to see him at that time. And because he was usually very gentle with discipline, I don't think he wanted to take action. He simply said, "I don't think you should do this." All the boys agreed and took the furniture back to the room.

On another occasion, Ellwood Evans somehow talked visiting professor Dr. Harry Ironside into letting class out a little early. Ellwood and some others needed extra time to pull off a stunt. They sneaked a firecracker-like little bomb under the hood of a student's car. When the student turned the ignition, the bomb went off and he took off running down the street.

I confess that I, too, pulled my share of jokes. When Ellwood got new stationery with his name printed on it, I dropped him a note saying how nice it looked. It was too bad that the printer had made such a terrible typographical error. Ellwood went crazy looking for the mistake, but he couldn't find it. He took the stationery to the printer, and everybody there searched for the problem. Ellwood became "carnally" frustrated and begged me to show him the mistake. It turned out that *Ellwood* was supposed to be in all capital letters, but the l's were in lowercase.

Although we seminary students realized that the study of theology is serious business, pranks and jokes provided needed relief from constant contemplation of the eternal and spiritual. Not a cruel bone was in the body of any student, but undoubtedly we all harbored a mischievous streak.

5

THE BEGINNING OF FULL-TIME MINISTRY

By bearing down on my schoolwork, I completed both my Th.B. and Th.M. degrees in 1934. Having arrived at seminary a year after me, Ellwood Evans received his Th.B. degree that same year and finished his Th.M. degree in 1936. Our story is worth telling.

Ellwood and I were football pals from Wheaton days. We used to travel from Wheaton to downtown Chicago, where on the street corners he practiced his love of preaching. He was very effective and always drew a crowd. Taking the electric interurban back to Wheaton gave him more opportunities to witness. When the interurban paused at a junction for a few minutes, Ellwood stood in the front of the car and said to the passengers, "I want to give you my testimony." Surprisingly, most people remained in their seats and listened politely.

His two-minute evangelistic message especially caught the attention of one passenger, a Methodist minister from Geneva, Illinois. The pastor soon invited Ellwood to speak at his church. It so happened that one of Ellwood's closest friends led the choir at that church. The friend had once said, "My organist is a nice, single Christian girl. I'd like you to meet her." At that time Ellwood didn't take his friend up on the offer. But when Ellwood accepted the pastor's offer to visit the church and to speak, he couldn't take his eyes off the organist, Harriet Lundgren. He was dumbstruck. They dated and became engaged, but they didn't get married until Ellwood finished his first seminary degree. I was the best man at their wedding on June 28, 1934. But the story doesn't end there.

At one of our Christmas breaks at DTS, Ellwood and I drove to Illinois in my car. I dropped him off at Harriet's home, where he would be visiting, and then I drove on home to Racine. After the holidays, I returned to pick him up. When I drove up to the house, Harriet's younger sister, Geraldine, came out to the car, and I met her for the first time. I can never forget the date and time: January 1, 1932, 8:00 A.M. Things would never be the same for me. Like Ellwood, I was dumbstruck! But at the time, Geraldine and I were traveling in different directions along certain "detours" in our lives. We were both going with someone else at the time, but about five years from the day we met, we got around our detours and started courting.

In a certain sense, we really didn't date because we were living a thousand miles apart. At the time we met, Geraldine was a student in elementary education at Northern Illinois State University in DeKalb. She was doing her student teaching in Geneva, about thirty miles away. Although we lived far apart, we wrote constantly back and forth for about a year and a half. We dated when we could, and our first date was to a literary society concert at Wheaton College. Geraldine recalls that I acted like a perfect gentleman and treated her like a lady. On June 28, 1939, exactly five years to the day after the marriage of Harriet and Ellwood, Geraldine and I tied the knot.

From our college days on, Ellwood was a great personal

friend. When Geraldine and I got married, Ellwood and I became close brothers-in-law. After seminary, Ellwood was pastor of several churches and even became the minister at Union Tabernacle in Racine, Wisconsin. He served there from 1941 to 1947. He also pastored in Oklahoma before he came to DTS to teach in the Bible department.

In 1934, years before my marriage, after receiving my two degrees at DTS, I decided to stay on there for my Doctor of Theology degree. About that time, responsibilities began piling up. In 1935, Dr. Rollin Chafer, Lewis Chafer's brother and the registrar and admissions officer at DTS, became terribly sick. His doctors told him that he must immediately give up his job as registrar. The position was dropped into my lap. As a graduate student, I already had a lot on my plate at the time.

I wasn't sure, though, that administrative duty at DTS was something in which I wanted to become more deeply involved. A year before taking that part-time registrar job, I'd started leading a small Fort Worth church, Rosen Heights Presbyterian, on a part-time basis. I'd wondered if I should become a full-time minister; that is, after all, the position most men pursue after their theological education. I'd heard of a small Presbyterian church in Colorado that was looking for a pastor, so I tried out for it. The folks were nice enough, but they showed little response to my candidacy and preaching. Then a great opportunity opened in Wyoming. A large company owned and operated a huge oil field and provided everything for its workers—stores, houses, and even a church. They dictated that the employees would have only one spiritual meeting house. The company owned the building, the pews, the pulpit, and the songbooks. Here was a pastor's dream! A midsize town of eight thousand workers with only one church—no competition! After I preached there, they extended a call.

But again the chemistry was just not right, and this time I was the one who bowed out of the opportunity. God was saying, "This is not what I have for you." Not long after that I was asked to be registrar. So I was "stuck" at DTS. Maybe administrative work and some preaching outside the school was God's plan for me.

Rollin Chafer was a godly man but he had little organizational ability. His filing system was a pile of papers jumbled on top of his desk. He had been performing several tasks without secretarial help, so it's no wonder that things were not in order. For twelve years, no grades had been recorded. It was spring when I temporarily took over, and the registrations for the previous fall had not yet been entered into the proper files. Rollin kept each semester's registration as simple as possible. When the students went to chapel at the first of the semester, he had them write on a piece of paper what they wanted to take. It was hoped that this little record (if you could call it that) would make it back to his office. It took three months for me to straighten out the mess.

That first fall semester while I was still acting registrar, there's no telling how many characters I admitted. Men simply applied to the school, and I'd let them in! I didn't know they were supposed to supply references or college transcripts. Surprisingly, to everyone else but me, that September we had a very large enrollment.

Then Rollin Chafer came back to his job and went back to doing things as before. President Lewis S. Chafer, however, seemed to like what I had done. He had earlier offered that position to me on a full-time basis, and he now renewed his invitation. Besides being registrar, he added, I would teach half of the theology courses. Now I was really under pressure because I was just a month and a half away from completing my doctorate. But I accepted anyway. Standing in his office, he led me in a very solemn prayer of dedication. As I was leaving his office, he shook my hand and promised a salary of one hundred dollars per month. I paid no attention to that because I knew that the school hadn't paid the faculty its full salary for years, although they tried to cover the needs of those with families. The first year, I received seven dollars and fifty cents each week. The second year, I was blessed with fourteen dollars each week. That went on through the Depression and World War II. In 1945, I started receiving a meaningful salary.

From the modern vantage point, the salary situation at DTS is amusing. But I also learned a world of spiritual lessons. In those early years, none of us who were involved in the seminary, or in any ministry, did so simply for the money. We were conditioned, in fact, to expect little compensation for what we were doing for the Lord. I didn't complain, and I don't know of many people who did. Now I'm not saying that it was right to receive little financial remuneration. After all, "the laborer is worthy of his wages" (1 Tim. 5:18). But, frankly, the money wasn't always available. Spiritually speaking, we felt as though we were millionaires, because we were very satisfied in serving Christ. God was performing miracles by keeping the doors of the seminary open on mere pennies. We could see where all of our efforts were going; capable men were being trained and going out to teach the Word of God in churches, on the mission field, and in Bible institutes. Those were precious days.

After becoming full-time registrar, I was able to work more closely with Dr. Lewis Chafer and be of more help to him. He was a great man of God and a deeply spiritual teacher. At about age fifty-five, he could not be expected automatically to be a great administrator.

As the school began to grow, a problem developed in regard to faculty. Although the school used many godly men who came and gave courses as guest lecturers, the need for full-time faculty had to be addressed. As early as 1929, Chafer realized that some difficulty existed in replacing regular faculty. It was increasingly hard to find men who held the doctrinal standards of the seminary. Chafer said to a friend, "I dislike to engage our own graduates, but, as a matter of fact, they are the best prepared men available at the present time." It was necessary to maintain not only doctrinal standards but also unity of theology. Rollin Chafer said,

> Nothing is more desirable in the teaching policy of a school of theology than consistent unity in presenting, in all departments of the curriculum, the beliefs and ideals for which the institution is reputed to stand. To secure this desired unity in presenting all phases of the truth we hold, the more recent additions to our faculty have been selected from amongst men of exceptionally high record in the Graduate School of our own seminary. (Archives, Dallas Theological Seminary Library)

In October 1936, the school filed for accreditation with the American Association of Theological Schools (AATS). That year, about sixty schools had formed this organization to create some kind of theological conformity. Although DTS was becoming known as a conservative school, Chafer didn't believe that this fact would hinder its chances of being accepted. On the horizon, however, was a push to modernize seminary curriculum as a prerequisite for accreditation. *The Christian Century* magazine (30 September 1936) published an editorial, "What Is Good Theological Education?" The article stated,

> One of the first projects of [this] new association is the restudy of the theological curriculum. It is to be hoped that, where it has not already occurred, the traditional Bible-centered curriculum may be replaced by a plan of study more balanced and comprehensive and more relevant to the needs of contemporary life.

By February 1938, it had become clear that DTS wasn't going in that direction. The hiring of faculty out of the pool of its own alumni did not conform to the policies of most accrediting organizations. We withdrew our application from the AATS, but by the spring of 1944, the seminary received accreditation from the State Education Department of the University of the State of New York. No compromise was required. Dr. Chafer could say, "The oldest and largest accrediting agency in the United States" has accepted DTS. One of the accrediting team members, Horace L. Field, wrote, "While not agreeing with some of the extreme views in theology of this group, they are the most earnest, hospitable group of college men and faculty I have met. . . . Taking everything into consideration, I feel this seminary is one of the very strongest seminaries scholastically in the country."

Besides his administrative duties, Dr. Chafer had other things on his mind. He was attempting to systematize dispensational theology and make it clear to the students. In doing so, he wanted especially to make clear the doctrine of the Church and the work of the Holy Spirit in this dispensation. The task of systemization would be an extraordinary undertaking, and he was breaking new ground most of the way. As he accomplished this goal in the clarity of the expla-nation of what the Bible actually teaches, I realized how I could help him, if he would let me.

Along with my many new duties, I also became Dr. Chafer's assistant in assembling his systematic theology so that it would reflect adequately the doctrinal teaching of the Bible. As his material was being taught in the classroom, he was creating copious notes that turned out to be one long dissertation in longhand. He composed the entire theology in about four years. Dewey Duncan, a conscientious secretary and a talented typist, then typed the manuscript. My job, then, was to divide all of that material into meaningful chapters. By 1947, we were ready to begin releasing it as a set. The first part was published in 1947, and the entire set was available in 1948.

His *Systematic Theology* had been an urgent concern with Dr. Chafer. He believed that most seminaries were failing to prepare men properly for the ministry, and *Systematic Theology* would be the heart and soul of what he desired men to learn in order to understand the Scriptures better. In the preface of the first volume, he said,

> The pastor and teacher must be trained for his leadership task. Under existing conditions this preparation is committed to the professors in the theological seminary. . . . If the pastor has no soul-winning passion, no missionary vision, is limited in his proficiency, and inaccurate as an exponent of the Word of God, his lack in these respects may generally be traced to the fact that he has been deprived of the God-intended, spiritual and vital training in the seminary. (*Systematic Theology*, p. ix)

Dr. Chafer never attempted to express his ideas in lofty, sophisticated language. He wanted his thoughts on theology to be understood; therefore, some critics charge that *Systematic Theology* is too simple and even incomplete. That criticism is patently unfair. His work has helped thousands of seminary and Bible institute students to understand theology, maybe for the first time. Missionaries and pastors were also blessed by its readability. No comparable theology written since has made the Word of God so clear. Maybe some theology texts have tackled certain complicated doctrinal issues with greater detail, but few have matched Chafer's eloquent yet down-to-earth explanations. I'm pleased to have been a part of that great spiritual undertaking.

Chafer's great strength was his stature as a man of faith in the Lord and of prayer. Many times he went to the Lord about financial needs, believing that to solicit outside financial support for the school showed a lack of trust in God. Except for a small bulletin printed about three times a year, no publicity was sought, no fund-raising drives were conducted, and no letters were written expressing needs.

I convinced him, finally, to write some letters to friends of the school. Often, money wasn't mentioned, but the point was made that the school was thriving, which caused many people to respond with financial help. Beginning in the fall of 1945, we began telling supporters of our needs. The year before we had raised only $36,000, and in 1945 we were $100,000 in the red. But by the Christmas of l945 we were able to meet our $50,000 budget and, for the first time, pay salaries in full. When I told Dr. Chafer that we could pay our teachers what they were due, he looked at me as though I were crazy. We've never missed a payday since.

Dr. Chafer believed, as do I, in God's sovereignty. We understood that the Lord could supply all of our needs without our having mentioned what those needs were. But I realized that the Lord desires to carry out His purposes by using the entire body of Christ. Mentioning financial needs brings other believers into the process of ministry, and the Lord uses those believers to supply what is needed. A careful reading of 2 Corinthians 8 and 9 will help those who are confused on this subject. At the time, Dr. Chafer was reluctant at fund raising, but later he was at peace about it and saw the wisdom of publicly expressing the seminary's financial burden in the task of training men for the ministry.

Because Dr. Chafer was a "softy" when it came to the students, years earlier he had proposed to the trustees that the school try to give the students everything free—tuition, room, and board. While discussing this at a board meeting, the trustees looked out the window to where the students' cars were parked. They noticed brand new vehicles with little evidence of poverty in view. They thought students could afford our modest fees. Still, the trustees tried to make it easy on the students. For room and board, they charged only enough to cover expenses.

In the spring of 1945, Dr. Chafer described what he called some disturbance of the heart. He wrote to a friend that it was "some involvement of the scarred tissue that I gained when I had my thrombosis." The scarring to which he referred had taken place nine years earlier. He admitted that he used to drive the work of the school, but then it began to drive him. In April, a stroke severely limited his work. At that time I became his official assistant. In order to accomplish what was important to the operation of the school, it was necessary to be even closer to him. His idea was to make me his acting chief executive. I told him politely that no such position existed in the corporate world. So he called me his assistant to the president, which was fine with me. I was learning a lot in the process of being helpful to him, and I knew that once he regained his health he would be trying to run things again. The board of trustees went along with his desire. They appointed me officially to the position of Assistant to the President.

On September 1, 1945, Chafer wrote what he called an "important notice":

> Dr. Walvoord is authorized to act as Chairman of the Faculty, Chairman of the Chapel and other public meetings, to act for and represent the President in all routine administration matters, to represent the office of the President in public as may be necessary, . . . and as far as possible to relieve Dr. Chafer of the load of administration detail. (Archives, Dallas Theological Seminary Library)

When Chafer returned sometime in October, he retained control, but he didn't have the same energy as before his stroke. Although I tried to be helpful, I was also frustrated because I had limited authority. He was not pushy, and he didn't have a possessive bent in his personality. But the seminary was, after all, his love, and I respected that. At one point, I determined to resign. When I approached him, he was so fatherly and loving that I forgot all about giving up the ship. To stay was the right decision, because the Lord still had me in training. What I learned from my experiences in the following years were invaluable in preparing me for what I would face.

But for Dr. Chafer's heart attack, I probably would have gone to Princeton to work on a second doctorate—this time in philosophy—which would have taken about two years to complete. Dr. Chafer had already written a letter of recommendation to Dr. L. P. Eisenhart, the dean at Princeton:

> It is my pleasure to commend to you Dr. John F. Walvoord. . . . Having been under my observation and in

close association for a term of years, I believe that Dr. Walvoord is one of the most competent young men of the
present generation. He is proposing to pursue studies in
Princeton University leading to the degree of Doctor of
Philosophy and I commend him to you most highly as being in my estimation unusually worthy of this privilege. (Archives, Dallas Theological Seminary Library)

But Princeton was not to be.

Because of veterans who were returning from World War II
during the late 1940s, enrollment at the seminary climbed,
reaching two hundred and fifty by 1952. Many of the enroll-
ees were moved spiritually by what they saw overseas, and
they wanted to return as missionaries to those foreign lands.
General Douglas MacArthur had, in fact, called for an influx
of missionaries to go to Japan. He knew what Christianity
could mean to that spiritually dark nation.

Although sometimes the students were okay financially
when they entered seminary, the veterans and their families
coming to seminary had it pretty tough. Most of them
struggled economically but believed that they were truly called
of the Lord. The seminary put up temporary housing for them,
but their living quarters were small, and the wives had to haul
their laundry to a washroom. With the little apartments
jammed together, privacy was a problem. Men came to class
with holes in their shoes and ragged coats. Material needs
were almost never completely met, but various churches gave
families clothes to get them through school. Many of the men
and their wives taught Sunday school for those congregations,
and the people went out of their way to help.

It was an unparalleled spiritual opportunity for the seminary. I can still see the eager faces of those men in the class-

room. Even more touching, I can hear them singing in the chapel with thanksgiving to the Lord. Because that was so long ago, many of those men finished their seminary training, served the Lord with faithful hearts in their appointed rounds, and have already been called home by their Maker.

In 1952, Dr. Chafer died suddenly, and an era came to a close. He had been a bridge between the older Bible teachers who spoke about the return of the Lord and a new generation that saw dramatic changes as a result of the war years.

With Dr. Chafer gone, I needed to make some decisions about my future. What was on the mind of the board of trustees and the supporters of the school? If offered the chance to replace him, would I want Dr. Chafer's job? Was I up to the task? True, I had helped him through the years, and I had seen his limitations. I also had seen his deep spirituality. What direction would the seminary take if I became president? But God is always in charge, and in time He would bring about what He wanted for the seminary.

An early picture of John Garrett Walvoord, Dr. Walvoord's father. He was an accomplished and respected public educator.

The Walvoord homestead in Cedar Grove, Wisconsin.

Commercial stores in Cedar Grove, Wisconsin, during the period of John's early years.

Early picture of downtown Cedar Grove, Wisconsin, taken around 1910.

Cedar Grove, Wisconsin, village meeting hall.

Winter in Cedar Grove, Wisconsin.

The interior of the Union Tabernacle in Racine, Wisconsin, where John first heard Arno C. Gaebelein and many other great prophecy teachers of the day.

The exterior of the Union Tabernacle, later named the Racine Bible Church.

The 1920s: Downtown Dallas about the time the Evangelical Theological College began.

Team of speakers for a Bible conference in San Diego, California, in the late 1920s. Dr. Chafer is on the right, with Dr. Harry A. Ironside next to him.

In October 1924, a ten-room colonial-style homestead was the first building to house the fledgling Evangelical Theological College, which later became Dallas Theological Seminary.

One of the early covers of The Voice magazine. Dr. William McCarrell led John to Christ in September 1925. Both Dr. DeHaan and Dr. McCarrell dramatically influenced John as a young would-be minister of the gospel.

The Wheaton College chapter of the Pi Kappa Delta Honorary Forensics (Debating) Society. John (second from right, back row) joined in 1930 when the team won eight out of their ten debates.

John played for three years as a Wheaton College football tackle. He was a "hard-hitting, fast-charging lineman."

At Wheaton College, John ran track and threw the discus. He was good enough to win yearly letters in sports.

Wheaton College track team, with John in the middle (back row).

Wheaton president Dr. James Oliver Buswell urged Walvoord to consider seminary training at Dallas Theological Seminary.

John about the time he graduated from Wheaton College and entered Dallas Seminary (1931).

John's portrait that he gave to Geraldine Lundgren upon their engagement (1937).

Geraldine Lundgren gave this portrait to John upon their engagement.

Wedding portrait of Geraldine and John, June 28, 1939.

Pastor Walvoord with the young group at Rosen Heights Presbyterian Church, Fort Worth, Texas, in the late 1940s.

Part of the outstanding faculty at Dallas in the 1950s: Dr. Charles C. Ryrie (l) and Dr. Merrill F. Unger (r).

The eleven-member Dallas Seminary faculty in 1949. Dr. Chafer is seated in the center. Dr. Walvoord is standing behind him.

As the president of Dallas Seminary, Dr. Walvoord addresses the first Christian Workers Conference in 1956.

Mrs. Walvoord served faithfully as Bible teacher, hostess, and spiritual "mother" to the wives of the seminary students.

The Walvoord children (left to right): John, James, and son Timothy with his new wife Dawn.

Son John with family: wife Jane, older daughter Currin, and baby Allison. John is a Dallas graduate: Th.M. (1967), Th.D. (1970).

Dr. Walvoord and Geraldine, his wife and invaluable spiritual partner.

Dr. Walvoord at 90 just as he began a seven-month weekly radio program teaching the books of Daniel and Revelation—yet again.

6

STEPS TO THE PRESIDENCY

Dr. Chafer had held a strange relation to the board of trustees. On one hand, they respected him as the founder of the school. But they seemed unable to act on certain matters that needed addressing. These men were godly business leaders, but they often didn't know how to make decisions on theological matters. When Chafer made known his opinion, they approved what he requested. As with most founders of great institutions, Dr. Chafer was pretty much a loner. While Dr. Chafer and the board got along, the trustees might sometimes have been uncomfortable with the way things transpired.

Earlier, Dr. Chafer had hinted to me that I might be his successor, but he didn't tell the board. Eight years before his death, about 1944, he had written a letter outlining all of the possible candidates that the board might consider if something happened to him. But he also included many reasons why those people should *not* be the president. His recommendation in the letter was that I become his successor. To my knowledge, he'd never before mentioned my name in this context, although I know he appreciated my management skills and knew that I agreed with him theologically. In 1944 I was not ready to be president of DTS. I was as green as grass and probably wouldn't have been the right man.

Nevertheless, Dr. Chafer's statement regarding me in the letter was most generous:

> In my estimation, Dr. John F. Walvoord is the greatest theologian, best qualified, among the younger men of the English-speaking world. He has written one of the best and greatest doctrinal books of this generation. He has written theological articles in each issue of our quarterly which have been just as valuable as any I have written. As a head to the department of Theology we have no other comparable to Dr. Walvoord. (Archives, Dallas Theological Seminary Library)

I'm humbled by his vote of confidence. I did my best to serve the Lord first and the school second.

When, in 1952, names of candidates were submitted for the presidency, the board wrestled with my name for more than two and one-half hours. Some trustees preferred other men to fill the position. Thus, their eventual offer to me wasn't the result of my overwhelming popularity. But in the end I was asked by the board to assume Dr. Chafer's position. Having been Chafer's right-hand man for so long, I may have seemed the obvious choice.

I was very unsure of myself. I wasn't recognized as a scholar because I didn't have copious publishing credits, plus I had my own image of what a seminary president should be—and I wasn't it! Although everyone at DTS had the best of intentions and were doing the best they knew how, the seminary was having problems, especially financial.

I accepted the position as president and soon discovered I had no authority to deal with financial matters. I also found that, rather than being a CEO, I was a figurehead who simply represented the school to the public. I reported my activities to the board and was reelected to my position each year. The tasks of administering the school remained largely in the hands of the board of trustees and the business manager, who reported to that group of men and not to the president. I did, however, have some authority as a member of the board of regents—the body that made educational recommendations and helped select faculty.

The Depression had been financially difficult for the school, and difficulties had continued into the period of World War II. At the time, the school had no firm policy in regard to handling donations and properly acknowledging contributions. This was a problem in 1952, when I became president, and it remained for eighteen years thereafter. I just had to trust the Lord, and be patient. In 1969, one of the most discerning members of the board at that time, General William Harrison, informed the board that the authority of my position should be upgraded. He urged the board to appoint me as chief executive officer, with authority to move the school forward theologically and at the same time make reasonable financial decisions to reinforce what we did in the spiritual realm. When the business manager resigned, his replacement was made answerable to me by a constitutional amendment. The problems inherent in my status began to be resolved, although it took some time to get everything operating properly. I was able to get more things done in five minutes than had been possible in five hours. With a more efficient chain of command, the seminary developed into a strong and influential institution of higher Christian education. After receiving its accreditation in 1969 from the Southern Association of Colleges and Schools, the seminary became dynamic. Several new structures, including the Cobb and Campbell buildings, were added, and student enrollment increased dramatically.

Three things prepared me to become president and to begin publishing theological volumes. First, the editing and writing work I did with Dr. Chafer on his theology books and on the school's journal, *Bibliotheca Sacra,* was most helpful. Second, while my involvement in the school was growing, I also served as pastor of a church, Rosen Heights Presbyterian, about thirty miles away in Fort Worth, Texas. Third was my further education in philosophy.

Churches are the vanguard of what the Lord is doing in this dispensation. People who are involved in training young people for ministry need frontline, trench-warfare experience. In a down-to-earth way, becoming a pastor gets one's hands dirty in doing the Lord's work. One need only study the letters of the apostle Paul to see that all is not perfect in local assemblies. Pastors must preach, teach, counsel, and put out grassfires. They must deal with people with a host of backgrounds and experiences. Pastors must encourage those who are growing spiritually but tolerate those who are immature. Thus, they must be patient with the carnally minded to turn them around in their relationship with Christ. Pastors must learn how to tell the truth but keep secrets, rejoice with the birth of the newborn but bury the dead, be emotional when it's called for but encyclopedic in knowledge of the Bible. Pastors must force themselves to mingle but learn how to hide in their studies and mine the gems of Scriptures. Pastors walk an imperfect walk but must model holiness in every facet of Christian life. As I became more involved in the seminary, the juggling of duties involved in being pastor of a church gave me an experience-based understanding of what the ministry is all about. Although I would later decide on major issues as president of DTS, I had to put those decisions in perspective as to what the seminary was all about. It was mostly about preparing men for the gut-wrenching ups and downs and pressures of ministering to the church of Jesus Christ.

That ministerial experience began when I was called to pastor the Rosen Heights church. It was 1934, the peak of the Depression years, and I labored part-time in that little vineyard for the next sixteen years. We began with sixty souls and ended up with between two hundred and three hundred. Since I was single when I became pastor, they started me out with a salary of seventy-five dollars per month. At the time, my mother was living with me, and we moved together to Fort Worth from Dallas. My mother's little pension of fifty dollars a month helped us make ends meet. We rented a furnished, five-room house for twenty-five dollars a month. For such low rent, the house had a few deficiencies. The roof leaked, and when it rained we put pans all over to catch the drippings. After one year, we moved to another house and again paid just twenty-five dollars a month rent, but this time the house was unfurnished. We gathered some odds and ends, but we splurged on a thirty-nine-dollar sofa from Montgomery Ward. That second house came along in 1935 when most people were struggling and had very little. I guess it was adequate for my mom and me.

The way my mother lived out her later years is interesting. In November 1932, when I was in my second year in seminary, my father was running to the train on his way to my grandmother's funeral when he suffered a heart attack. He lingered for about one and a half years. He and Mother had been married for thirty-three years when he departed for heaven. She never remarried, living until 1974, when she died at the age of 101. She was a widow longer than she was married.

I had to provide a little better for Geraldine than I had when Mother and I were living together. Being a thrifty Dutchman, I had saved a little money, and so had Geraldine. In 1939, we

pooled our funds to sink all three thousand dollars into building a little five-room house in Fort Worth. I was fairly talented with tools and later added on two upstairs rooms. With
Geraldine's help as pastor's wife, things continued to grow at
the Rosen Heights church.

I believe that we went through all that a couple serving the
Lord might experience. Sometimes we were blessed, and at
other times we wanted to give up. But the farther one walks in
Christian service, the more one learns to expect both the good
and the bad. By keeping our spiritual eyes on the Lord and
His Word, and by believing that we are in His will, we begin
to see everything in proper balance.

When I accepted the call to the Rosen Heights church, some
people said that I wouldn't last very long. The church had
fired the previous man. But we stayed for sixteen years, plus
an additional year as they searched for a replacement. The
people in the congregation who listened discovered that my
passion was to preach the Bible. I always taught an ongoing
series on doctrine. I covered every major doctrine I thought
was crucial to the spiritual growth of the church. On Sunday
evenings, I taught, verse by verse, through different books of
the Bible. In the years at that church, I went through the New
Testament one and one-half times and about half of the Old
Testament. I think that my ministry could be characterized as
steady and, in the long term, successful. Some people might
not have thought it spectacular, but it was consistent in pre-
senting the truth and thorough in covering the Word of God.

About the time I began working with the church, I went on
radio station KRLD with evangelist and teacher William
Hawkins. We did a weekly broadcast that lasted for well over
fifteen years. Hawkins was a brilliant pioneer and one of the
first preachers to understand the power of broadcast media.

He was also great to work with. He gave me almost unlimited freedom to do what I wanted on the program. Geraldine joined in helping me. We'd get up every Tuesday morning around four A.M. and go to the station for the program in Fort Worth. She played the organ, and I taught through the Bible on those early morning radio studies. Obviously, I had my plate full of ministry opportunities that were covering a wide field of service. With all that was beginning to happen to me, I felt humbled. I saw no need to get in a race with other men in Christian ministries.

In today's churches, something different seems to be going on. Many pastors think they must compete with other ministers who might have more talent or rhetorical flash. They pressure themselves to outperform the leaders of larger churches. But the Lord hasn't called us to competition—He has called us to faithful obedience. That's an important lesson for today's young preachers. If they don't learn early on what God is doing with them, they'll burn themselves out, both emotionally and spiritually.

When the Rosen Heights church originally started, the church leaders went to Fort Worth Presbytery to ask if it was permissible for premillennial eschatology to be taught in the church. The presbytery said yes, so I taught the blessed hope of the Rapture, the Tribulation, and the bodily return of Christ for His kingdom. When I left, the church called an ordained Princeton Seminary graduate who was a protégé of Dr. Donald Barnhouse, who was strongly premillennial and expositional in his ministry. Barnhouse was also outspoken in his denunciation of liberalism. The church was in pretty good shape doctrinally, and it had more than twenty thousand dollars in a building fund.

However, for some time members of the presbytery had

considered that they had made a mistake in permitting premillennialism to be taught. When Briggs left, the local presbytery swept in and took over, moving the elders aside and putting their own liberal teachers in the pulpit. They also took all of the Bibles out of the pews. Because many Sunday school classes and the youth group were still teaching premillennialism, they were abolished. Then the presbytery heaped upon the church the final insult: the pastor was given the only key to the building. Most of the people were closed out of the affairs of the congregation. But the Lord keeps His Word going. Those who left that church began Northwest Bible Church in Fort Worth, which still exists.

From the actions of that presbytery, I realized that satanic opposition is always hanging over the heads of churches. Satan desires to destroy the work of God; he hates the solid teaching of the Word. Thus, pastors and elders must remain doctrinally vigilant. Paul warned the Ephesian elders, "Be on guard for yourselves and for all the flock, among which the Holy Spirit has made you overseers, to shepherd the church of God which He purchased with His own blood" (Acts 20:28).

That third step that helped me to be an effective president of DTS was pursuit of an M.A. degree in philosophy. When I started teaching seminary courses in 1936, some of the students seemed to lack respect for my academic credentials because they thought I didn't understand history or any other discipline beyond theology. Philosophy majors occasionally taunted me because I didn't understand the field. So, in 1942, I decided to do something about it. I went to Texas Christian University (TCU) in Fort Worth for a degree in philosophy.

When I first began to study philosophy, I was afraid that it might affect my Christian faith. I soon discovered, however, that, although philosophy raises some penetrating questions, it has no final answers. I also found that for every major philo-sophical question, the Bible has the final answer. The Word of God ends up intellectually strengthening one's faith.

Looking back on all that I was already doing, I must have been crazy to take on the work involved in attaining another degree. At DTS, I was registrar, admissions officer, and dean, teaching half of the theology courses and working almost full time as a pastor at Rosen Heights. I had to prepare fourteen times each week for some kind of ministry work, either teach-ing or preaching.

I faced a disappointment when I first entered TCU. For some reason having to do with the war, they said that I couldn't major in philosophy. They insisted that I study southwest Christianity, of all things. I plowed ahead and took a lot of history courses, except ancient history, which I had taken al-ready. For some courses, I merely had to take the exams with-out being in the classroom. I studied for and took exams on eighteen hours of history. Then they decided that I could major in philosophy.

In the History of Philosophy class, three of us were funda-mentalists. When the other two men (one was Oliver Price, later a DTS student) challenged the professor, he became an-gry and tried to sink all three of us. I learned to challenge him by simply asking questions. At one point, he made a sweep-ing statement on a specific discussion about the Bible saying, "Christ never said this." I quoted the verse to him in which Christ indeed said just that. The professor stood there in the class slightly stunned. Finally he said, "You're right." Suddenly, he did a 180-degree turn in the way he treated me. When I made an *A* on his exam, I think his opinion of me went even higher. He created special courses to get me through the stud-ies more quickly. My final paper was on *Hume's Essay on*

Miracles. Hume's work on this subject covered only about twenty-five pages, but I ended up writing a thesis on the subject that was one hundred pages long.

I did advance academically from my work at TCU. Because I thought that I might later work on a Ph.D., I took German and French. I'm not sure if the work at TCU was beneficial to what I would ultimately do for the Lord, but I guess no harm was done. And I learned some interesting lessons from the degree in philosophy. Studying all that the scholastic world has to offer in liberal theology or in philosophy as opposed to Christian faith has only confirmed my belief that liberalism has nothing to offer, and that both reason and faith support conservative theology.

My M.A. studies, too, broadened my view of the world and of history, which prepared me for the books that I would later write, including *The Millennial Kingdom* (1959). I felt more confident doing the research on the millennium and, because I had become more sensitive as to why people thought the way they did, I became more adept in seeking out clues as to why many of the later church fathers turned against the doctrine of the millennium. The courses in history and philosophy gave me better insights into the growth of the church and a better grasp of the mistakes made by the theologians of the time. I saw how Augustine, for example, turned the literal view of prophecy into allegory. He separated prophecy from other Scriptures as if it required a separate principle of interpretation. Through my studies I became able to defend more adequately the history and development of premillennialism and dispensationalism.

Some people might think that becoming pastor of the Rosen Heights church and earning an M.A. in philosophy were but sidebars to my career at the seminary. But I can now see how

God dramatically used these experiences to prepare me for what was to come.

And the time for a defense was rapidly approaching.

7

THE WAR OVER FUNDAMENTALISM AND PREMILLENNIALISM

I started writing on doctrinal issues in the 1940s. In the 1950s, I felt led to write books to help Christians understand the Bible. I didn't necessarily set out to defend premillennialism or dispensationalism, but I felt compelled to make the whole counsel of God clear. And that counsel certainly included issues related to the return of the Lord and to dispensationalism.

When I enrolled at DTS in 1931, skirmishes occurred over premillennialism but not dispensationalism. Because dispensationalism was a tenet of fundamentalism, in our circles those issues were pretty much cut and dried. In the 1920s, the great controversies between fundamentalism and liberalism took place. By the 1930s, the winds of liberalism had won out in several denominations and many seminaries, and then dispensationalism became a crucial issue. Until then, dispensationalism was well accepted. In fact, up until the 1930s one could be a dispensationalist in the Presbyterian church, although not everyone agreed on the issue, especially the amillennialists. Thereafter, some denominations began an all-out war on their churches that remained fundamental and conservative. Liberal speakers and teachers were sent to those churches to challenge what was being taught. It was soon discovered that those in the congregation who opposed liberalism were carrying *The Scofield Reference Bible* and that those who knew something about their Bibles were dispensationalists. Dispensationalism then became the target of rebuke.

In the 1930s, most of the liberals who went on the attack against dispensationalism didn't know what it stood for, but they still attacked it as heresy. In truth, the attack was against not only dispensationalism but also fundamentalism, premillennialism, the virgin birth, and other doctrines that can't be compromised. That trend is still around today. The most vicious attacks leveled against dispensationalism are from those who sense that it is a conservative belief.

Throughout his life, Dr. Lewis Chafer was clearly fundamentalist and conservative in his teaching of the Word of God. He never departed from this position. But he was concerned about some of the extremists in the fundamentalist movement. At a time when the leaders of that movement were making extreme charges that were alienating many people of fundamentalist persuasions, he believed that, under the guidance of the Holy Spirit, the school was bringing in some of the best Bible teachers in America who were independent of radicalism. Dr. Chafer wanted to build a seminary of the highest standard, apart from any organized body within the radical movement. I think he accomplished his goal.

The view of Dr. Chafer was that everyone was a dispensationalist. To demonstrate his point, I spent the time surveying one hundred systematic theology textbooks, most of which were postmillennial or amillennial. I found that fifty percent of them had a positive view of some of the dispensations of the Bible. Even postmillennialist Dr. Charles Hodge, in his much-respected *Systematic Theology,* holds to four dispensations and even defines them as I would define them. That dispensationalism is held as a common doctrine was also true among many postmillennialists and amillennialists of the last of the nineteenth century and the first part of the twentieth century.

Dispensationalism is the doctrine that God places moral requirements upon a specific era—or dispensation—of history. God's command to Adam in the Garden of Eden that he not eat of the forbidden fruit became such a moral requirement. The same thing can be said of the dispensations of conscience, human government, the period of the Law, and on through the Church Age and the dispensation of the kingdom.

Dispensations, however, are not theological divisions imposed upon the Scriptures. The heart and soul of dispensational teaching is literal interpretation, that is, a normal hermeneutic that leads one to take the Word of God at face value. If one does that, the dispensational differences that are clearly presented in the plan of the Bible become evident. One doesn't have to fully understand all of the theological ramifications of dispensationalism in order to identify them.

Dr. Chafer used to say that all evangelicals are dispensationalists. If you don't go up to Jerusalem every year and offer sacrifices, you're a dispensationalist. You understand that the church is not under that economy. If you're not stoned for picking up sticks on Saturday, you're not under the dispensation of the Law. That was a different period with a distinct legal requirement that had been placed upon the nation of Israel. In the Church Age, we rejoice that we're not under the bondage of the Law. Although the Law was from God and was in itself good, no one could abide by it. Because of the weakness of human flesh, it was a heavy burden to bear. Thank God we're now living under the dispensation of grace, because none of us could morally maintain the legal system of the Law. God is now operating in the world on the basis of the finished work of Christ on the cross. He has moved the world into another dispensation.

By taking the Bible at face value, we observe several truths. We discover a pretribulational Rapture, a terrible period coming called the Tribulation, and the return of Christ to reign and rule in Jerusalem for one thousand years. But when World War II came along, some dispensationalists and premillennialists jumped the gun. Some of them saw the war as the first part of the Tribulation and thought that the Second Coming was to take place soon. They flirted with a mid-tribulation teaching and went so far as to spiritualize that event. Current events, however, should not color how we view Scripture or cause our doctrinal beliefs to shift.

The birth of the nation of Israel in June 1948 was, of course, important. That event set the stage for the end times. But believers must observe what the Bible lays out as the prophetic timetable. Teaching should not be adjusted to fit newspaper headlines. But at the same time, certain trends in the history of our times have prophetic overtones. It is difficult to understand how amillennialists can say that they see no significance in the return of the Jews to Palestine.

Another conflict between premillennialists and amillennialists is whether the church inherits the promises given to Israel. The term *Israel* is used nowhere in Scripture to indicate either the Church or the Gentiles. When amillennialists hear us teach about the coming kingdom among the Jews, they don't appear to understand. In their theological thinking, God is through with the Jews.

When certain prophetic passages about Christ's return to reign in Jerusalem were showed to one prominent Reformed theologian by his dispensational friends, he admitted that he had no firm alternative interpretation. He seemed to be set in his ways and remained an amillennialist. He refused to accept the literalness of the Bible on the issue of the millennial kingdom of Christ.

As the events of World War II unfolded, Dr. Chafer was satisfied about the seminary's position on the doctrine of the Rapture. He wanted, though, to solidify the views on the grace of God and on the Church. But I thought that we needed to focus more on what the Bible taught on the Rapture and the Tribulation. We needed to be positive about what the Scriptures said and to make our position clear.

My concern in regard to these matters was well founded. What had been happening in regard to fundamentalism and dispensationalism in the Presbyterian church up to the 1950s brought about a turning point in my life. It was very personal, yet it made me realize the confusion about prophetic issues and the teachings of dispensationalism. In the 1930s and 1940s, the leaders in the Southern Presbyterian denomination never confronted me or called me a heretic as a result of my dispensationalism, although they were progressively turning against that view. While a pastor in the Rosen Heights church, I was a member of Fort Worth Presbytery. By 1950, I had become heavily involved with the seminary and decided to move to Dallas. But the presbytery in Dallas didn't like the school and ruled that DTS's doctrinal focus wasn't acceptable to their way of thinking. Because I had no intention of leaving the school, I would have to resign from membership in the presbytery. I asked for a letter of transfer to the Independent Fundamental Churches of America. But instead of giving me that letter, the presbytery simply struck my name from the role and refused to issue that document as they normally did for transferring pastors. They tried to get me upset, but I wouldn't budge or be intimated. They even offered me the pastorate of a large Presbyterian church in another area if I would leave the seminary. This confusion and turmoil went on for a year, but they finally gave in and sent a letter of dismissal with approval. This was a victory for me. I hadn't wanted to resign from the denomination in protest in the first place; I wanted to leave in good standing. The antagonism wasn't over, however. One of the Presbyterian churches in Fort Worth wrote in their paper that I had been kicked out because I was one of those speckled birds that believed in *The Scofield Reference Bible*. It was not true, of course, that I had been kicked out of the Presbyterian church. I left in good standing. Because of my attachment to the seminary, I didn't have many regrets. Whether I was Presbyterian in church government didn't make that much difference because, after all, the school wasn't Presbyterian. But because of my association with the seminary, I wanted my ordination to remain valid.

With so many theological misconceptions, controversies, and disagreements within denominations, there was much to say about what the Bible really teaches. I felt the time was ripe to write some books, though I was certain whatever I wrote would be criticized.

I'm often asked how I responded to criticism. It has never bothered me, especially if it is for holding to the truth. People have consigned me to the pit for my dispensational beliefs, or have said that I was inspired by the Devil for holding to the doctrine of eternal security. I used to answer negative letters. And sometimes I still write a response if I sense in the writer's tone that he or she might learn something from me. But for the most part, I simply reply with a kind but short letter and point out to the writer that we have a disagreement on a certain issue.

Sometimes the controversy takes a different turn. For example, in the fall of 1945, while Dr. Chafer was convalescing from his heart attack, Dr. John R. Rice attacked Chafer's book *True Evangelism*. The book originally came out in 1911 but was reprinted later by Moody Press. For a time, Chafer was a traveling evangelist. He knew what issues were important in seeing people come to Christ. In *True Evangelism*, Chafer posited that evangelism is the work of the Holy Spirit and that human tactics and methods can hinder an honest decision by the lost. He always asked people to pray for the unsaved. To attack the book, Rice got a group of pastors to sign a petition and even tried to stop the printing of the reprint. It is ironic that in *True Evangelism* Chafer addressed the arm-twisting tactics of some evangelists. He was against pressured altar calls, though he practiced reasonable methods to give the lost person a chance to express trust in Christ. He would say from the pulpit that those who wished to inquire more about salvation should come down front and meet with him afterward. Sometimes a hundred or more people came forward after the service to profess their trust in Christ.

To further his attacks on *True Evangelism*, Dr. Rice used his paper, *The Sword of the Lord*. Moody considered removing the book from publication, and in June 1946, Rice continued his attack in his paper by publishing all of his correspondence with Moody Press. He even turned on Moody Bible Institute. Dr. Chafer wanted to answer Rice, but I persuaded him to say nothing. Moody wrote to us that they saw no problem with what Chafer had written, but under pressure from Rice they discontinued selling the book. They claimed to have lost fifty thousand dollars during the controversy.

Sometimes it takes the influence of godly men to turn things around. A good friend of the seminary and a generous supporter of Moody Bible Institute, Mr. T. J. Mosher, wrote a three-line letter to Moody asking them to reconsider. They responded and began selling the book again. It went from sales of three hundred copies a year to an amazing six thousand copies a year. In time, Rice ceased his attack. Years later, his son-in-law wrote glowing endorsements of DTS in their paper. Rice was a great defender of the faith, but I believe he misunderstood Dr. Chafer's thoughts on evangelism. By remaining silent and not provoking a war among the brethren, I believe we did the right thing. As the old saying goes, sometimes you have to "let go, and let God."

Dr. Chafer once wrote to another man who was under fire that he should "just quietly go on stating the truth" and pay no attention to the attack. In the letter Dr. Chafer said that Dr. C. I. Scofield had told him, "Never descend to controversy. You have no time or strength for it. Give out the positive truth. There is nothing that can stand in front of it." This advice became my philosophy as well.

The seminary drew fire sometimes for its doctrinal statement. But the statement also received praise. Many groups approached us to ask if they could use it. We replied that the statement was copyrighted but that a church could adapt it for their own use. We were willing to grant permission to use the statement in any way but the seminary's name might not be associated with it unless the statement was quoted exactly in its current form.

It's certainly possible for a doctrinal statement and position to be misunderstood. A professor from another seminary wrote to me asking a question concerning our view on the authority of the Bible. He thought that we should emphasize that Christ is our authority. I wrote back that, in regard to Scripture, the orthodox view is that the Bible is our written authority. We all recognize, of course, that Christ is a final authority, but that the Holy Spirit is the divine Author of Scripture. No one would deny that ultimate authority is with the Lord. But the Bible is our ultimate authoritative book that gives us light about spiritual matters. Such misunderstandings must be handled with biblical authority and with patience and gentleness.

8

THE PUBLISHING YEARS

I cut my writing teeth when I helped prepare Dr. Chafer's eight-volume *Systematic Theology* for publication. Chafer had written his material on small sheets. He then recopied and divided the work by subjects, after which I assisted him in making chapter divisions. All of that began with his original teaching notes from years earlier, which had to be adapted to books.

Because of my experience in helping Dr. Chafer edit his *Theology,* and because of my involvement with *Bibliotheca Sacra,* I felt I was ready to share my own thoughts about the Word of God in book form. *Bib Sac* had given me opportunity to publish my thoughts on various theological subjects. Previously published by the Presbyterian seminary Pittsburgh Xenia, and also by Princeton Seminary, it was one of the oldest journals in America. For some time, the subscription list had consisted of about three hundred subscribers, and it was a dying publication when DTS took it over in 1934. Dr. Rollin Chafer edited it from 1934 to 1940. I assisted with the journal for some time and became the editor in 1952. I wanted to see the journal used to perpetuate sound biblical theology, and in time I think that happened. After many years of editing the journal, I realized that I had more to do than I could handle. It was time to turn the work over to someone else. Dr. Roy Zuck had been an assistant editor on the journal, and he was the associate editor from 1974 through 1986. In July 1986, he became the senior editor when Dr. Don Campbell became president of the school. By then, Roy was an extremely confident editor who showed great competence.

Besides writing many articles in *Bibliotheca Sacra,* I wrote, edited, and co-edited about thirty-one books. Again, my main purpose was to be positive and to explain the Bible as I understood it.

I realized that no satisfactory work, aside from Scripture, was in print that presented all of the essential truth about the Spirit of God. Many people were not clear on His work during the Church Age. Thus, my first book was *The Holy Spirit,* a compilation of articles I'd published in *Bibliotheca Sacra* and classroom notes that I had prepared for my course on the Holy Spirit. To help clarify the confusion about the nature and work of the Holy Spirit, I wrote,

> If . . . the church [can] be defined as the saints of this age only, the work of the Holy Spirit in baptizing all true believers into the body of Christ takes on a new meaning. It becomes the distinguishing mark of the saints of the present age. (*Holy Spirit,* p. 138)

In 1943, I bought the type from the early printings and published it myself. Fifteen hundred copies were printed; I sold them for $1.50 each.

Because so many attacks were being made against the doctrine of the Rapture, my next work was *The Rapture Question,* first published by Dunham Publishing Company in 1957. That material, too, was first published in *Bibliotheca Sacra*. Other material from *Bib Sac* was put in *The Millennial Kingdom* (Dunham, 1959). Since premillennialists were becoming more literal in their interpretation of prophecy, I wrote in the preface,

> This [literalness] has tended to sharpen the distinction between those holding that the Rapture of the church occurs before the Tribulation and those who hold that it follows the Tribulation. . . . If the current events indicate that the end of the age is approaching, the question as to whether the church is to be raptured before end-time events are fulfilled becomes more important than ever. (*Millennial Kingdom*, p. 7)

Other books would follow.

Over four years, Zondervan Publishing House released *Israel in Prophecy* (1962), *The Church in Prophecy* (1964), and *The Nations in Prophecy* (1967), publishing the trilogy as one volume in 1988. These books were written to explain that the Lord had different purposes for Israel, the Church, and the Gentile nations. Many Christians confuse Israel and the Church, seeing them as somehow melding together, or envisioning the Church as replacing the Jewish people. It's true that the current Church Age is made up of both Gentile and Jewish believers, but the dispensation of the Church is a distinct period with distinct purposes. That uniqueness is generally overlooked. God clearly lays out His plans for these three entities; to confuse them leads to doctrinal error.

To help students of the Bible understand certain prophetic books of Scripture, I wrote a series of commentary volumes: *The Thessalonian Letters* (Dunham, 1955), *The Revelation of Jesus Christ* (Moody, 1966), *Daniel* (Moody, 1971), *Philippians: Triumph in Christ* (Moody Press, 1971), and *Matthew: Thy Kingdom Come*

(Moody, 1974). Because most of these commentaries continue to be published, I must have struck a positive nerve. These books shed light on difficult prophetic passages by explaining them in the context of the specific Bible books. Daniel's seventy weeks (Dan. 9:20–27), for example, is best explained within the flow of the entire book of Daniel. The commentaries give clear exegesis, so that scholar, pastor, and the person without formal theological training can grasp what the Word of God teaches. These volumes also give perspective and explain where we might be today in the grand scheme of things. Of the remarkable Bible prophecy in Daniel, I said,

> It may be concluded that Daniel's great prophecy of the seventy sevens comprehends the total history of Israel from the time of Nehemiah in 445 B.C. until the second coming of Jesus Christ. . . . With Israel today back in the land, the fulfillment of these prophecies may not be too long distant. (*Daniel*, pp. 236–37)

Because many have been confused about even the first coming of the Lord Jesus, I wanted to help students of Scripture grasp a dispensational understanding of the Gospels. My commentary on Matthew explores such doctrines as law and grace, which are often not explained properly. At the Lord's first advent, was He offering the Church or the prophesied millennial kingdom? Was the kingdom postponed? Is the Second Coming literal or allegorical? Is the Church now the kingdom? And is the prophesied messianic kingdom yet to come? To answer these and other questions, I wrote that the book of Matthew

> proceeds to account for the fact that Christ did not bring in His prophesied kingdom at His first coming. . . . [Matthew]

was designed to explain to the Jews, who had expected the Messiah when He came to be a conquering king, why instead Christ suffered and died, and why there was the resulting postponement of His triumph to His second coming. (*Matthew: Thy Kingdom Come*, pp. 12–13)

One of the books I wrote that challenges all students of prophecy, no matter what their view, was *The Millennial Kingdom*. I drew upon my understanding of history and philosophy. *The Millennial Kingdom* sets forth the views of postmillennialism, amillennialism, and premillennialism. The tone of the book is not negative and is meant to help anyone who's confused about eschatology understand the great differences in how Bible teachers relate to prophecy. The book compares the various beliefs, explaining the origins and development of the three conflicting opinions. I'm convinced that Bible students who honestly set aside their preconceptions about prophecy and take the prophetic Word at face value will arrive at premillennialism. One of my graduates in fact noted that *The Millennial Kingdom* explained better than had any other book published the issues regarding these theological systems, as well as the hermeneutics involved. He commented, "We're in a war over interpretation." In the book, I wrote,

If the earthly reign of Christ can be spiritualized, so can His resurrection, His miracles, His second coming. Modern liberals can justify their denial of literal resurrection by use of the same hermeneutical rules that . . . [are used] for denial of an earthly millennial kingdom. (*Millennial Kingdom*, pp. 66–67)

I also wrote books on theological issues besides prophecy. Along with the *The Holy Spirit* textbook, I wrote *Jesus Christ*

Our Lord (Moody, 1969), *What We Believe* (Discovery, 1990), *Major Bible Prophecies* (Zondervan, 1991), and *The Prophecy Knowledge Handbook* (Chariot Victor, 1990 [later published in 1999 as *Every Prophecy of the Bible*]). I was editor or coeditor of many other volumes, such as the *Bible Knowledge Commentary,* Old and New Testaments in two volumes (Scripture Press, 1985, 1983). I also revised and edited Chafer's *Systematic Theology* to an abridged, two-volume edition (Victor Books, 1992), *Truth for Today* (Moody, 1963), and *Inspiration and Interpretation* (Eerdmans, 1957).

Besides his *Systematic Theology,* Dr. Chafer's *Major Bible Themes* has had a significant doctrinal impact over the years. That material initially came out in note form around 1924, but it was first printed as a single volume in 1926. In 1953, the seminary took over the rights to the book, but in the early 1970s, I thought that it needed some revision, and additional doctrinal subjects were added. Zondervan published *Major Bible Themes* in its new form of fifty-two chapters in 1974. The added chapters actually came from many of the doctrines with which Dr. Chafer had dealt in his *Systematic Theology.* What makes *Major Bible Themes* such a blessing is that it can be used in schools, churches, or simply as a helpful doctrinal guide for personal use. It is used in hundreds of churches and dozens of Bible colleges as a basic doctrinal textbook. Considering how long the book has been around, imagine the thousands of people who have been blessed by studying it. I think that the Lord will continue to bless this important teaching tool for years to come.

Chafer had high expectations for *Major Bible Themes* when it first was published. In the introduction, he explained why he thought that the teaching of Bible doctrine was so important:

The divine purpose is that the servant of Christ shall be
fully equipped to "preach the word; be instant in season,
out of season; reprove, rebuke, exhort with all long suffering and doctrine." These chapters are published with the
prayer that they may honor Him whose glory and grace are
supreme, and that some among the children of God may
be helped more accurately "to speak the things which become sound doctrine." (p. 10)

How the Lord leads in the conception and publishing of a
book is an interesting story. Before writing *The Holy Spirit at
Work Today* (1973), for example, I went to California in 1971
for the Torrey Lecture Series, which was dedicated to shedding
light on important doctrinal issues. I presented five lectures on
the work of the Spirit of God. After writing out a series of notes
on the subject, I delivered the same material in a teaching series at the Central American Mission School in Guatemala City.
The missionaries were delighted, and the notes became a book
that was later translated and published in Spanish. Eventually I
sent the manuscript to Moody Press. I thought that the book
was needed to help people understand the practical and personal way the Holy Spirit works within us. About that time, the
seminary was looking for a give-away book, so I wrote back to
Moody, telling them that if they printed this work, we would
order six thousand copies. They agreed. When the volume was
printed they ran an additional five thousand copies and sold
all of them in a matter of two weeks.

But the story keeps going.

The president of Moody Bible Institute decided to make
the book a premium on the Moody radio station. Thousands
more copies were printed and sent out as gifts. Then a representative of the radio program "Back to the Bible" wanted the

book to give away on their broadcast. They ended up ordering eighty-five thousand copies. In one year, the book had reached one hundred thousand paperback copies sold.

One of my best selling books was *Armageddon, Oil and the Middle East Crisis.* The book was half finished when the 1973 Yom Kippur War broke out. I sent the first half to Zondervan and asked them if they wanted to print it. I got a letter back that said, "We've got the type set on what you sent. Where's the rest of the book?" My son John, who is a pretty good writer, jumped in and helped me finish that project. Although he was working on a Ph.D. at Columbia University, he put in the time to polish it for publication. Zondervan did full-page ads in magazines. The first printing arrived at the bookstores in early 1974. Six hundred thousand copies were eventually printed in English, and I believe that between three hundred thousand and four hundred thousand were finally turned out in other languages.

When the war was over, and the oil embargo was lifted, the book went out of print. But then the Gulf War came along in 1990, and interest in the Middle East and Bible prophecy rose again. Zondervan printed a revised edition of 1 million copies in English and sixteen other languages. Around 2 million copies were printed, although not all of them sold.

Not long ago, I was speaking at a private school commencement in Prestonwood Baptist Church in Dallas when a woman about forty years of age stopped me in the aisle. She said, "I read your book *Armageddon* and got saved!" Just like that! I felt so gratified because my goal was to explain prophecy to the unsaved. The response was amazing. Whole families, as well as people trapped in cults, came to the Lord. As I wrote page after page, I would say, "If what I'm saying is true, you should consider Christ as your Savior." In the preface, I put it thus:

It is hoped that those who read this volume will be attracted to Jesus Christ as the only Savior and Lord and will have an intelligent understanding of how history is moving on to its climax. (*Armageddon*, p. 16)

I concluded by writing,

Our present world is well prepared for the beginning of the prophetic drama that will lead to Armageddon. Since the stage is set for this dramatic climax of the age, it must mean that Christ's coming for His own is very near. If there ever was an hour when men should consider their personal relationship to Jesus Christ, it is today. God is saying to this generation: "Prepare for the coming of the Lord." (*Armageddon*, p. 228)

Then, at the end of the book, we included a gospel presentation of the plan of salvation. If we know of dozens or even hundreds who turned to Jesus as their Savior, there are likely many more about whom we don't know. What a privilege it will be when we get to glory and see the great company of believers whom we were instrumental in touching for Christ's sake. We don't see all of the results of our labor here on earth, but the Lord keeps good ledgers. We will someday realize that we didn't serve Him in vain here below.

Of all my opportunities to touch people through publishing, one of the greatest occurred when in the late 1950s, I was asked to join a prestigious committee of eight other dispensationalists and fundamentalists to work on revising the notes of *The Scofield Reference Bible*. By the 1920s, Oxford Press had sold millions of copies of the Scofield Bible. To head the new revision committee, Oxford Press asked Dr. Schuyler English, editor of the notes on the *Pilgrim Bible*, which had limited circulation. Wilbur Ruggles, the author's representative of Oxford, didn't think nine fundamentalists could work together on such a project. He expected an emotional tug-of-war among the men, but it didn't happen that way. We all got along, and every decision on all reference revisions was unanimous.

Let me explain our procedure. The whole committee went over the Bible and listed changes to be made. The changes or corrections were duplicated for the entire committee to look over. The corrections were then discussed at the next meeting, and each change was assigned to one committee member for a rewrite. To ensure that the theology was clear, we often wrote certain notes entirely from scratch. When this was done, the changes were brought back to the entire committee for a reading. Altogether, the changes circulated four times before they were finally approved as they had been altered. The material was then turned over to three men and Dr. Frank E. Gaebelein, who spent a couple of years checking the notes carefully. They went over the material many times, from Genesis to Revelation, to ensure that every detail was right. When our work was sent to the publisher, they spent about a year double checking everything thoroughly.

As the serious work on the Reference Bible progressed, we had some light moments. Whenever a question arose about something in the Hebrew text, Dr. Charles Feinberg and Dr. Allen A. MacRae whipped out their Hebrew Bibles and debated the matter. On another occasion, Dr. Wilbur Smith said he had never thought of the Angel of Jehovah as being the person of Christ. Most of us on the committee had long before accepted this.

We added perhaps fifty percent more references to ensure that future readers would clearly understand the meaning of the Word of God. When the original version was compiled it was nearly impossible for a busy man such as Dr. Scofield to explain every important chapter in the Bible. The book of Ezekiel, for example, had chapter after chapter without any meaningful notes. We thought that important commentary ideas had to be added. The revised version came out in 1967, and it was extremely successful, having been read by millions since its publication. Oxford Press paid us, but the amount wasn't great. The men on the committee, though, didn't do the work for pay. They believed in the Reference Bible because all of them had through the years seen the blessing that it brought to thousands of hungry Bible readers and students.

Writing Bible notes, commentaries, and theological textbooks are excellent ways in which Bible teachers are able to extend their classroom influence to hundreds and thousands more. The works themselves provide an opportunity for the serious student of the Word to focus on what is written, to go back and read again, to look up verse references, and to share a book with someone else who is spiritually thirsty. Some purists argue, "We need to study only the Bible!" While this is certainly the ideal, the Lord says that He gives teachers to His Church, and they are to help others understand scriptural truth. The apostle Paul writes that God has ordained truth to be "entrust[ed] to faithful men, who will be able to teach others also" (2 Tim. 2:2). When Paul was first brought to the city of Antioch, he and others stayed there for an entire year, met with church members, "and taught considerable numbers" (Acts 11:26). Antioch became the first seminary where the Word of God was explained. Schools such as DTS continue this tradition of learning in our day.

9

EARTHEN VESSELS

I've known great men of God through the years. None of them was perfect, yet many of them blessed me and touched the lives of thousands of laymen, pastors, and students. Several of these men came to Dallas Seminary over the years as faculty or guest faculty. I taught at Bible conferences with some of them. Each of these men had not only his gifts and talents but also his own limitations.

All of us are but earthen pots (2 Cor. 4:7), a little cracked but still useful to God in His mysterious plan of reaching the world for Christ. We all have deficiencies, but we also have gifts given to us by the Lord. This is true of the men in this chapter. Although I could list many more who have been vital to the work of the Lord and the ministry of the seminary, I mention just a few here.

Henry Allen Ironside (1876–1951). "Harry" Ironside was one of the most prolific Bible teachers of the past century. He entertained people with humor and love, although he once said, "I'm not an entertainer; I'm a preacher." On one occasion, my graduating class of fifteen students all gathered at Dr. Chafer's home and were enthralled by Ironside's antics. Because he was an avid reader and had a keen mind, he spent two hours in recitation from passages he'd read in books. Yet he was a humble man. He could talk to the influential and relate to the lowly, all at the same time.

Dr. Ironside would come to the seminary and spend one month, teaching as many as three classes. He gave us that time each year because he loved the school, although there was another reason. His son John lived just down the street from our campus. John had been wounded in World War I, was a shell-shock victim, and struggled to control nerve problems. He nevertheless founded Southern Bible Training School, which later was named Southern Bible Institute and continues to have an effective educational ministry for African-American pastors.

Dr. Ironside was born in Toronto, Canada. He never went beyond the eighth grade, but he was very intelligent and taught himself the Bible. He was also influenced by many of those early dispensationalist teachers.

Some insensitive students came to him and asked, "Why do we have to go to seminary? You didn't."

He answered, "The Lord uses a lot of people who never had the opportunity for school. But I've never known a minister to amount to anything who had that opportunity but refused to take it."

The students loved Dr. Ironside, but he was popular with everyone who heard him speak. He wrote some excellent devotional commentaries that are still published.

He was visiting his half-sister in New Zealand when he went home to be with the Lord.

William McCarrell (1886–1979). As mentioned earlier, in my youth McCarrell had a profound influence on the path I was to take. He was a graduate of Moody Bible Institute, and in 1941 he received an honorary doctorate from Wheaton College. Among his many accomplishments for the Lord, three stand out. He helped establish the Independent Fundamental Churches of America in 1930. Before that, he founded the Cicero Bible Church in 1913 and built the congregation up to a membership of fifteen hundred. During the 1920s, he was a daring moral and spiritual force against Al Capone and other gang leaders, who were headquartered just blocks from the Cicero church. He spoke out against speakeasies, brothels, saloons, and gambling dens, and he developed a taskforce of evangelistically fervent laymen (called the Fishermen's Club) who conducted street evangelism and visited jails. Among the converts were some of Capone's henchmen. Although McCarrell never came to teach at Dallas Seminary, he spoke at our chapel on at least one occasion, and he served on the faculty at Moody for many years.

Carl Armerding (1889–1987). An outstanding Plymouth Brethren teacher, Amerding taught at the seminary as a visiting professor from 1945 to 1949. But since the school often didn't pay a full salary, he resigned and went on to teach at Wheaton College. He frequently returned to the seminary as a guest lecturer.

He was a stately and fastidious man who was always well dressed. Although he was not formally trained, he knew the Bible and was well received at the school and in conferences. Although I'm sure that he had his lighter side, when on one occasion we misspelled his name in one of our bulletins, he let us know about it.

Dr. Armerding's love for the Lord and for the Scriptures was evident in the way he took his audience to spiritual heights with his teaching. He was a blessing to people for many years, and continued teaching until he was ninety-five. His son, Hudson Armerding, served as president of Wheaton from 1965 to 1982.

Charles Feinberg (1909–1995). Dr. Feinberg was a brilliant scholar who was from an intellectual Jewish family. At the age of six, he was reading Hebrew. Around the time he received his B.A. degree from the University of Pittsburgh in 1929, he came to Christ. He and I entered seminary at the same time. In fact, we roomed just across the hall from each other in the single-men's dorm. He was able to accelerate his work at the school, receiving both the Th.B. and Th.M. degrees in 1934 and his Th.D. in 1935. Being the scholar that he was, he went on to Johns Hopkins and received his Ph.D. degree in Old Testament and Semitic Languages.

Feinberg had a great love for the Old Testament and the Hebrew language, and he wished that all of the students had the same passion. He gave volumes of homework in Hebrew translations, making it tough on the students. We were proud of him as a professor, but he left DTS to go on to a higher calling, becoming dean at Talbot Seminary in California from 1952 to 1979. His book *Millennialism: The Two Major Views,* first published by Moody Bible Institute in 1936, was a classic explanation of the difference between premillennialism and amillennialism. In the forward to the second edition, Dr. Alva J. McClain, former president of Grace Theological Seminary, wrote, "Since 1936, it appears that the proponents of the [amillennial] system, by their increasingly *anti*-millennial attitudes, have more clearly than ever provided ample justification for Dr. Feinberg's main thesis." Feinberg was on target in understanding the forces aligned against premillennialism in that early period.

J. Vernon McGee (1904–1988). McGee went one year to Dallas but believed that, because he was a Presbyterian, he needed to finish at a school in that denomination. He went to Columbia Seminary to finish his bachelor degree, but then came back to Dallas and completed his Th.M. (1937) and Th.D. (1940) degrees. While he was finishing his schooling, he was pastor of the First Presbyterian Church in Cleburne, Texas. Then he moved to Pasadena, California, where he was pastor of the Lincoln Avenue Presbyterian Church. Later, he was called to the Church of the Open Door in Los Angeles, where he served for decades. I had the privilege of speaking for him in that church. He started his radio programs, which became so well received that his recorded programs continued for years after his death. His radio transcripts were also turned into a popular and practical commentary series.

Although I had known him for years through the seminary, I got to know him well when we taught together at prophecy conferences. Once we spoke in Decatur, Georgia, where he had received his bachelor degree. He seemed very nostalgic about the area and his experiences while a student. As we drove over the mountains and through the dales where he had preached in country churches, he lit up at being back in a place of which he was so fond.

Dr. McGee would often come to DTS to teach special courses. Although the students loved him as a teacher, he didn't have much use for small talk. Students tried to engage him in conversations, but he generally wouldn't respond. To return the favor of his coming to teach for us, I went out to his church for conferences.

At one such conference, about five hundred people came each weeknight to hear the various speakers. When McGee spoke, many more showed up. But McGee decided to close the Friday evening session, fearing that only a handful would come. Earlier in the week I had announced that I was going to speak on the subject "Will World War III Occur before the Rapture?" Moaning a bit, he relented, and we had the service.

We were all shocked when 1,500 people came to hear the message. Often, it's difficult to know what people will respond to, but they generally accept what the Bible says about Bible prophecy. Therefore, prophetic issues still draw many who want to understand what Scripture says.

Wilbur Smith (1894–1977). Smith possessed an incredible knowledge of biblical and theological literature. He was a bibliophile who had skimmed or read thousands of volumes. He claimed to have read every commentary in print on the book of Romans. But Dr. Harry Ironside, no slouch when it came to books, wouldn't let Smith get away with that. Ironside teased and pressed Smith, asking if he'd read such-and-such a commentary on Romans. Smith finally conceded in regard to a certain title, "I never heard of that book!" Ironside loved it! He was delighted when he could occasionally stick a pin in a balloon.

Once when Dr. Smith and I were at a Bible conference in New York, I was assigned to speak on Revelation 16:12, one of the toughest passages in the book: "The sixth angel poured out his bowl upon the great river, the Euphrates; and its water was dried up, that the way might be prepared for the kings from the east." To prepare for my presentation I read through one hundred commentaries, coming up with fifty different interpretations on the verse. Later, what I discovered on the passage was published in a book that I'm sure Smith had read. By a strange turn of events, he was assigned to teach on that same verse at a later conference we both attended. He got up and said, "I don't know anything about it and nobody else does either." Then he said he had a most wonderful revelation about another subject. He discovered that there was both a millennial hope and an eternal hope! In truth, most people were already familiar with that belief.

Despite humorous moments, Smith was a good man who loved the Lord. A prolific writer, he was in demand at conferences and for years had a much-respected ministry across the country. He also wrote a regular column about books in *Moody Monthly* magazine, and he once brought some special lectures to Dallas.

When Smith spoke and wrote, people took interest. Dr. William Culbertson of Moody Bible Institute once said, "You know, if I say, 'It's going to rain today,' nobody pays any attention. But if Wilbur Smith says, 'It's going to rain!' the whole country gets alarmed."

Smith did, however, have one pet peeve. He had little patience with crying babies in the audience when he was speaking. On one occasion after he got up to speak, he said, "I want everybody with babies to leave the room. I don't want any babies crying while I'm talking." You can imagine how unpopular his statement was with young mothers! I think that day we lost some in the crowd who had come to hear him.

Smith eventually taught at Fuller Theological Seminary. He had a great love for Dr. Chafer. He once wrote to a friend,

> I do not believe there is any man in America today who, . . . has made such a profound contribution to the theological education of young men, especially in equipping them with a love for the Word of God, and a knowledge of how to properly expound it, as Dr. Lewis Sperry Chafer. . . . We have in this beloved man a master teacher and a pioneer in theological education. (Archives, Dallas Theological Seminary Library)

Merrill F. Unger (1909–1980). Unger received his Th.M. (1943) and Th.D. (1945) degrees from Dallas. A great scholar and a deep thinker, Unger wrote a brilliant dissertation, "Biblical Demonism," that eventually was published by Scripture Press. The work was so scholarly that many people in the medical community read it. Unger so loved the Old Testament that he later received his Ph.D. (1947) in Old Testament Hebrew and Semitic Languages from Johns Hopkins.

When Dr. Feinberg left the seminary, we asked Unger to take the position teaching Hebrew. This provided an opportunity to change how the courses were taught. Feinberg was intense and driven by his love for the Hebrew language. While he was teaching with us, I discovered that the students were using about fifty percent of their study time on the Hebrew assignments. We asked Unger to examine the course requirements, and if changes were in order to make them. He agreed with our assessment that the course requirements were excessive and cut the intensity of the studies in half.

Dr. Unger was a lovable person who deeply loved the Lord. The students said that his prayers at the beginning of class seemed to last forever. But the students also discovered that Dr. Unger could be easily sidetracked. If they weren't ready with their lessons, they led him off track with questions that had nothing to do with their assignments. Dr. Unger's tests, though, could be very tough. A final exam consisted of only four questions from any paragraph in the entire textbook. One of the four questions on an Old Testament Survey course was "What is the London Polyglot?" After what seemed to be hours of pondering, one freshman gave up and answered, "The London Polyglot is a collection of old Egyptian vases in a London museum." Since that question was one-fourth of the grade, the student received a D for the semester. (The London Polyglot was actually a 1669 folio of ancient texts consisting of Hebrew, Aramaic, Syriac, Samaritan, Ethiopic, and Arabic, with a separate Persian vocabulary and a comparative Semitic grammar.) The student failed to see the humor when Unger wrote on his paper, "Nice try!"

Besides his books on biblical demonology and Old Testament introduction, Unger wrote a Bible handbook, a well-received dictionary, textbooks on both Old and New Testament archeology, and a small but important book on the gift of tongues. In 1981, he published a large two-volume commentary on the Old Testament (Moody). All of his books sold well. He was an incessant writer and was extremely capable as a wordsmith. When traveling on a cross-country automobile trip, he often wrote in a notepad on his lap while his wife drove. The story is also told that when he stood in line waiting to get a ticket at the airline counter, he jotted down ideas for a new book.

Through the years, I've had the privilege to serve the Lord with many such men. I observed their limitations, but God uses imperfect people because there is, after all, no other kind. He uses people I might have passed up for one reason or another. On one hand, we should strictly apply principles of the Bible in evaluating character. On the other hand, we should show grace and mercy. I've always tried to live out Romans 14:10, 12: "Why do you judge your brother? . . . We shall all stand before the judgment seat of God. . . . So then each one of us shall give account of himself to God."

Unless it is necessary to make a judgment for some urgent reason, it is best to remember that the problems of others are not always our business. We are all sinners, and the Lord takes people with blots and uses them. Nothing is impossible with God.

10

IMPORTANT DOCTRINES FOR CHRISTIAN LIVING

Nothing is more important than to explain to the lost how one becomes born again. But often today, the gospel is not made clear and little teaching tells how to live the Christian life. Most pastors give plastic bandage sermons that are simply devotionals. In some churches, members could attend all of their lives and just get little bites of truth, like eating hors d'oeuvres. They never get a full meal. Several reasons exist for the failure to convey both the clear gospel message and what it means to live as a Christian.

First, pastors in America and elsewhere are simply not able to expound the Bible. In most seminaries, students receive survey courses on the Old and New Testaments, but they are not taught—that is, given exposition on—the whole Word of God. Thus the graduates leave unqualified to teach.

Second, I don't think that the average minister makes the gospel plain. Every sermon must include the gospel and how to be saved. Dr. W. A. Criswell, the pastor of the First Baptist Church in Dallas, said he goes into the pulpit with the assumption that twenty-five percent of the people in a given audience are not born again. As a young man, I would have been included in that number. I was brought up in a church where the gospel wasn't made clear. Many people in the pews are, I'm sure, just like I was; they simply don't understand the gospel. Therefore, our churches are full of non-Christians. They might be religious, but they're not saved.

Third, after people accept Christ as their Savior, they often do not get follow-up discipling. New Christians must understand how to become sanctified in their daily walk with the Lord. The Bible must be taught and then applied for Christian living. Without this step, new babes in Christ have a hard time growing to maturity. Many churches fail to help new converts learn what God expects of them as His children.

Fourth, many Christians do not understand the significance of prophecy. Prophecy should be explained and taught from the pulpit and in the Sunday school classroom, but too much silence exists on the subject. Some years ago, I spoke at a Bible conference in Canada. Many people in the audience were from large churches that were not necessarily fundamentalist in theology. A significant number of people, however, were hungry for the teaching of the Word. After I spoke on the Rapture of the church, a middle-aged woman came up and said that she had never heard this doctrine taught before, and the last time she had heard a prophecy message was when she was a teenager. The trend to neglect prophecy is puzzling, because one-fourth of the Bible is prophetic in nature. In other words, people aren't taught great portions of the Scriptures. Prophecy is not only important in telling believers what is coming upon the earth but also is an evangelistic tool. I've seen many hundreds, if not thousands, of people accept Jesus as Savior when the entire prophetic plan, from eternity to eternity, was explained. The doctrine of the Rapture is especially important because that event removes the child of God from earth just before the terrible events of the Tribulation. This is why it's called the "blessed hope."

Not only is the Rapture misunderstood, or not taught at all, but many other truths are not emphasized. Although I'm known as a teacher of prophecy, and I love to explain the return of Christ, I feel a duty to teach other doctrines as well:

Jesus as Savior. Christ is the Savior. He is the Redeemer. This is our message. The entire gospel pivots on the fact that Christ died for our sins. If He's not our Savior, we don't have anything. That Jesus has saved us is the central doctrine of faith. He is our Savior in that right now He is our intercessor before God the Father. And He's going to save us by removing us from this sinful world and taking us home to be with Him.

The Holy Spirit. He is the third person of the Trinity, possessing all of the attributes of God. He indwells every believer. The Spirit is the key to the spiritual life. In the positive sense, the Christian is to walk by the Spirit, but the Christian must not grieve or quench Him (Eph. 4:30; 1 Thess. 5:19). Most pastors tell people that they must live better, but they leave out how to do it. They fail to explain the work of the Spirit and don't show how He aids the believer in daily living. In addition, many pastors don't explain the sanctifying power of God's Word or the intercession of Christ. It's one thing to tell people to be good but quite another thing to tell them how.

Gifts of the Spirit. The Bible tells us that the gifts are distributed sovereignly. The choice is not up to us. Some gifts—such as the gift of prophecy or tongues—are no longer needed. Although some gifts may have been temporary, certain gifts are still with us, such as teaching, administration, exhortation, and evangelism. I've heard Bible teachers claim that they personally have special revelation to predict details of events in the future, but no one can go beyond the Scriptures in predicting what is coming.

We can, however, look to the Bible for guidance and illumination. I firmly believe in the healing power of God, but spiritual healing through the laying on of hands in the New Testament era was a token and an attesting sign that the Lord was working through Christ and the apostles. God today gives different gifts to different people, and the Lord uses those gifts through the power of His Holy Spirit.

The Sovereignty of God. God is in charge. We have to bow to His will in all things—even things that we don't desire. We must say with the apostle James, "If that's the Lord's will, that's what I will accept" (see James 4:13–16). The ideal is to be completely yielded to God and let Him direct our lives.

Unconfessed Sin. Holding on to known sin grieves (Eph. 4:30) and quenches (1 Thess. 5:19) the Spirit. To walk with the Spirit (Gal. 5:16) is to take one step at a time with moment-by-moment dependence upon Him. You can't put off your trust of Him for tomorrow; you must trust Him today. Many Christians are not listening to God or confessing their sins (1 John 1:9). When we've sinned, we have to open the door, receive forgiveness, and start walking in the light (v. 7). That's doing the will of God.

Some people teach that, because our sins are covered by Christ's work on the cross, we don't have to confess our sins. But the Bible says that we should, although we don't have to beg for forgiveness. We shouldn't question His willingness to forgive: "He is faithful and righteous to forgive us our sins and to cleanse us from all unrighteousness" (v. 9). For our part, we have to face up to what's wrong and admit that we've sinned. This very process is used by the Spirit to keep us from continuing in sin.

Repentance. Although the word *repentance* often carries the thought of "sorrow," the New Testament focuses on the meaning, "to change the mind." The word *metanoeo* is used often in the Gospels to refer to the way the Jews related to Jesus. The Jewish people had rejected Him, refusing to acknowledge that He was their Messiah. John the Baptist urged Israel to *repent*—change the mind—and put their faith in Christ. So the word is generally used as equivalent to belief. But some people today say that you must be sorry for sin. We should, of course, feel contrition for our waywardness, but it must be understood that sorrow does not secure salvation. God the Father is satisfied only with the work of His Son on the cross. Not even our grieving for sin will move God to save us. Judas Iscariot felt sorrow for betraying Jesus, but that didn't help him gain personal salvation (see Matt. 27:3–5). So often, people want to help God along in providing salvation, but it can't be done.

The Rapture of the Church. John Darby receives the credit for explaining this doctrine. He was one of the most vocal nineteenth century teachers to realize that the church is not Israel. As this became clearer, it became more obvious that passages teaching about Christ coming to receive the church referred to a separate event than passages about His coming to earth to reign. Although the early church didn't fully understand the Rapture passages, they did acknowledge that Jesus would come down to earth to establish His messianic rule. Thus the early church was clearly premillennial. But by the second century they were abandoning literalness on the Rapture and were accepting the allegory of the Alexandrine school of thinking. They failed to see the difference between the Rapture and the Second Coming of the Lord, and they never resolved their confusion.

Strangely, the church fathers were both pretribulational and posttribulational. They believed in the imminent return of the Lord, but they also saw Him coming back after the church had gone through the Tribulation here on earth. On these and many other issues, the church fathers were not always right.

I met one man who said, "The Rapture verses in First Thessalonians 4:13–18 are not hard to believe." I agree, but some people are so opposed to this doctrine they say, "Even if it's in the Bible I won't believe it!" To me, the idea of going to heaven is very comforting. Or if the Lord returns today, how wonderful that will be! Some people, however, are a little afraid of meeting the Savior. But the Scriptures teach us that being with Jesus in heaven is far better than the life we have here.

I was just thinking this morning, what if today were the day. The Rapture is a precious truth to me, and I think that it should be constantly in our minds that He could come today.

The Kingdom. How we view the millennial kingdom might not affect how we live the Christian life, but it does affect how we interpret approximately one-fourth of the Bible. An amillennialist might be spiritual and an excellent soul-winner. It's a short step, however, from allegorizing or spiritualizing prophecy to doing the same with the deity of Christ or the Virgin Birth. Such a departure in a seminary or a church doesn't usually happen suddenly but over a period of decades. This is what happened to some of the great amillennial seminaries of the past. Their nonliteral approach to prophecy cast a shadow over other areas that they once held as literal, actual happenings, such as the Creation, the Fall, and the Flood. If all of the prophecies about the return of Christ can be taken in a spiritual sense, then so too can the creation story and the story of the worldwide flood. Unbelief in one area leads to unbelief in another area. Only if one accepts the Bible as literally true, has one started out on the right track.

Some time ago a great controversy took place over the doctrine of the inspiration of Scripture. Good men holding all kinds of views on prophecy came together and held several conferences in order to reinforce this important truth. But as they talked with each other, they ended up disagreeing over issues of interpretation. They all agreed that the Bible was the inspired Word of God, but those who were not premillennial didn't accept large portions of its prophetic message as literal. More heat than light was produced.

The Bible becomes subverted in three ways: (1) by denying that it's inspired, (2) by denying that it's literal, or (3) by simply disobeying it and not following what it says.

The Gospel and Evangelism. I've been asked what's most effective in leading people to Christ. First, people must learn that they are lost. When I was fifteen, although I was religious, I didn't realize that I was lost without Christ. When people realize that they are not saved, the next question is how to get saved. This is where the convicting work of the Holy Spirit comes in. From the human standpoint, we have to teach that Christ died for our sins on the cross. This act made it possible for God to offer redemption as a gift. To be a gift, it has to be received as a gift; we can't earn it. Jesus said, "The one who comes to Me I will certainly not cast out" (John 6:37).

I always tell people, "If you're not saved, there is just one reason. It's *not* simply because you're a sinner, for we are all sinners. It's because you haven't come to the Cross." This fact must be made plain to the unsaved. Prophecy, too, can play a dynamic part in evangelism. The subject can comfort those who have trusted Christ as their Savior, and it can awaken the lost to the fact that they're not ready. In the 1970s, the Lord used Campus Crusade and DTS graduate Hal Lindsey to explain the truth of future prophetic events to thousands of students on college campuses. Through the Scriptures, Lindsey used prophecy to turn many atheists and agnostics to the Lord. Many thousands of people were converted.

The gospel, then, should be given in every public sermon. When someone comes to hear us speak, he or she should be able to learn how to be saved, even if that's not the main point of the message. Evangelism should always be forefront.

The Cross. The Roman practice of crucifixion was a terrible way to die. Yet Jesus suffered that horrible death because He loved us. Thus the cross is the symbol of our Lord's sacrifice. His death, however, was no accident. God poured out His wrath on His only Son and, by accepting this sacrifice through faith, we can have peace with God.

In the Christian life, we too have our crosses to carry. We have to endure many hardships that we don't want to go through. But we should not expect this life to be free of tension and problems. As the Father gave to His Son grace to endure the pain of the cross, so He gives grace to us to bear the trials that come upon us.

The Blood of Christ. The shedding of Christ's blood was evidence that He was dying on the cross. Theologically, His blood speaks of His sacrifice, and it cleanses us from sin. Some people think that His blood is now kept in heaven, but that is not indicated by Scripture. Jesus went to heaven *through* the blood, not *with* the blood. The blessing, however, is that because of the shed blood of Christ, we are forgiven. God is satisfied that the debt of our sins has been paid.

Grace. The doctrine of the grace of God is fundamental to our faith and differentiates Christianity from all other religions. All other beliefs are legalistic, requiring adherents to try hard at being good and then somehow to earn their way into God's favor. But grace is given to us freely because Christ died for us. God gives us what we don't deserve—blessings—and those come about because of His grace.

One of my favorite verses is Ephesians 2:8: "For by grace you have been saved through faith; and that not of yourselves, it is the gift of God." This verse summarizes the gospel—that salvation comes entirely by grace. By its grammar, the verse indicates that the entire process—grace, salvation, and faith—are all the gift of God.

Mercy. As an aspect of the love of God, mercy comes from grace. Because the Lord pities people, He withholds the punishment for sin. But He can't be capricious in His mercy; the cross of Christ makes mercy possible. Although the Bible says that we reap what we sow, mercy and grace intervene. If we had to pay the full price for what we've done wrong, we'd all be in serious trouble before the Lord.

Justification by Faith. The heart of the salvation message is that we're not only forgiven but also justified. Justification, then, is a crucial doctrine of the Word of God and means that righteousness is imputed to those who are in Christ by the baptism of the Holy Spirit. God no longer sees us in our imperfections, but in the perfection of His own Son, based on His work on the cross. God declares us righteous, not because we are righteous on our own merits, but because we are united with Christ.

Faith. The word *faith* means that we have trust in God and believe in Him and in all that He does. Faith is as simple as that.

Worship. I think that the use of rock music to stimulate emotion in church is misguided. That type of emotion is of the flesh and not of the Spirit. I personally like some jazz music, but it does nothing to help my spiritual life. Some time ago, I was at a banquet at a big church where they had turned the music over for the evening to a very contemporary musical group. When they began to play, people whooped it up and danced in the hall. Listeners might like the music and it might even be performed well, but if the music and the feeling it invokes is carnal, spiritual growth will not be engendered. When we get to heaven, I don't think we're going to be worshiping with jazz or rock music.

Some churches go to extremes trying to be contemporary. Many independent churches that were once bastions of Bible teaching are becoming so concerned about attracting people to their services, they've put their hymnbooks in the storeroom.

But other churches go the opposite way. Some years ago, I was invited to speak on the Sunday before Labor Day at a big church located in a college town. A thousand people were at the early service, and they were singing some of the old choruses and hymns of the faith. Everything was pretty traditional. Twenty-three hundred people, mainly college students who had come out—on a holiday weekend yet—to hear the Word of God, were at the next service. Again, the service was largely traditional. At the evening service only about seven hundred people were expected. More than fifteen hundred attended! I asked some of the folks who were there, "What is the secret to the church?" They answered, "We don't go in debt, we heavily support missions, and our pastor is a good expositor of the Word of God."

Giving. In the New Testament doctrine concerning the church, the tithe, or tenth, is not required in giving. That was mandated under the Old Testament as part of the Law. In this dispensation, however, we are to give one hundred percent of ourselves. Everything we have belongs to the Lord, but it's as if He gives us an allowance because we need something for ourselves in living this life. If we have available means, He doesn't want us to live in a hut or drive a car that's falling apart. It's okay to have some nice things, and that's illustrated often in the Bible. We shouldn't spend our resources foolishly because it all really belongs to the Lord. But some missionaries and many Christians living in backward lands are in desperate need and lack financial support. If believers have the ability, they should share with those who have a need, or support the ministry with more than a tithe. They should give twenty to thirty percent—or more!

Peace with God. In reference to salvation, Christ becomes our Peacemaker by His sacrifice on the cross. Paul writes, "He Himself is our peace" (Eph. 2:14). And for the Christian walk, the Holy Spirit imparts peace. As Paul says, "The fruit of the Spirit is . . . peace" (Gal. 5:22). Christian bookstores are full of books about how to find peace, but a book can't give us peace. It's a supernatural quality and is given as a gift. Being anxious in this life is not what Jesus wants for us. He told His disciples, "Let not your heart be troubled; believe in God, believe also in Me" (John 14:1).

Forgiveness. God forgives us as part of salvation. Thus, we should forgive others (Eph. 4:32). The doctrine of forgiveness is even mentioned in the Lord's Prayer. Christians are not to hold grudges.

Prayer. We communicate with the Lord and He communicates with us through prayer. Consider what the apostle James wrote: "You ask and do not receive, because you ask with wrong motives" (James 4:3). I don't want that to be said of me. I ask the Lord for big things all of the time, though not all of what

I request is given to me. I've seen prayers answered dramatically in regard to things needed at the seminary. We will someday look back and know that many prayers were answered in ways that we did not expect or even realize (Eph. 3:20).

The Supernatural. God usually works through normal and natural means to accomplish His purposes. If, for example, you're sick and you pray, the Lord might use a doctor to heal you. That's not exactly a miracle. But if you're sick and He has to invade or "bend" His normal laws, that's a miracle. I believe that God works through both natural and supernatural ways. But a miracle has some theological significance—there are spiritual reasons for what occurs. Miracles do occur, but *supernatural* does not necessarily mean "miraculous." I believe that God's providence is by definition supernatural. Thus the supernatural is part of the Christian life. We're not expected simply to live naturally; we're expected to live supernaturally. The new birth that starts our journey as Christians is a supernatural event. We're supernaturally sustained, and we have a supernatural future. In these ways the supernatural is normal for believers. The apostle Paul said, "We look not at the things which are seen, but at the things which are not seen; for the things which are seen are temporal, but the things which are not seen are eternal" (2 Cor. 4:18).

Holiness. Another word for sanctification, *holiness* means to be set apart for God's use. God can use a dollar bill or He can use an ordinary person. A lot of things can be used distinctly for the Lord.

Humility. We should not think of ourselves more highly than we ought to think. But humility is a two-sided coin—we are children of the King because Christ died for us. In that sense, He lifts us up and, in Christ, makes us someone. But Paul asked, "What do you have that you did not receive?" (1 Cor.

4:7). So whatever distinguishes us—brains, ability, education, achievement, or gifts—it doesn't give much ground for pride, because God has given all these to us. He made each of us with particular abilities, so we must discover who we are as made by God. He molded us, and we belong to Him.

Death. Death is simply the cessation of life on earth. When we die, we go directly to heaven and into the presence of the Savior. But Jesus could come for us today, and we would leave this earth without facing death. Paul put it perfectly when he wrote, "We are of good courage, I say, and prefer rather to be absent from the body and to be at home with the Lord" (2 Cor. 5:8).

Heaven. This is where we go after we're raptured or after we die. Heaven is in the very presence of God. I think that we'll have some wonderful surprises there, and I look forward to it because it's a much better place than is earth.

Rewards. We've been privileged to serve the Lord, and for this we will be given badges—perhaps not medals worn on our chests, but they will be some form of recognition that we, as His servants in this life, served Him. Rewards might be like those given for playing football; we're to be rewarded as to how we played the game. Our goal, however, is to hear the heavenly Father say, "Well done!"

Seminary Students. Although this topic is not a doctrine, I feel a sense of responsibility to speak a word here in regard to seminary students. They see the need to serve God and they train to improve their gifts. Seminary students are a fine lot, but they're not perfect. Sometimes their ambitions are to serve in the big church, but that might not be the Lord's will for them. I was a student at one time, but I don't believe I wanted the big church. I just wanted to go where God directed me. Some seminary students might dream of being a great leader, but they will have to grow up, and that can be a painful process. Some students get discouraged or have personal problems and then drop out. When they do that, Satan wins. And that's a tragedy for the ministry of the gospel.

11

THE CLOSING DECADE
OF THE TWENTIETH CENTURY

I'm often asked what changes I've seen since I retired in 1986. People wonder what dramatic shifts I've observed in both the culture and in evangelical churches.

In some ways, no changes have occurred. Although people and institutions come and go, the same problems exist today as always. Having said that, I am concerned about the growing lack of emphasis on the fundamentals of the faith—salvation, sanctification, and the teaching of prophecy. There's silence, too, on eschatology and the blessed hope of the coming of the Lord. Prophecy conferences are no longer popular. All of this may not mean a change in doctrine, but a shift in emphasis certainly has occurred. And that shift can soon lead to a downgrading of doctrinal truth.

The teaching of doctrine is like the waves of the ocean; interest on certain subjects rises and wanes. Although I teach more than prophetic messages, the theme of the return of the Lord is my specialty. And I note that fewer and fewer ministers are teaching on the Rapture, the Tribulation, and the coming kingdom. Pastors claim that these subjects are controversial, but I contend that the problem isn't opposition but ignorance on these subjects.

The rapid strides toward a more secular world indicates that we're approaching the time of the Rapture. Some people are hoping for a spiritual revival, but the Bible doesn't indicate this will occur. Instead, the Bible indicates an increase of apostasy. And, in fact, many seminaries and churches are departing from the faith. The majority of seminaries in America neither accept the inerrancy of the Bible nor hold to the literal interpretation of prophecy. If the Scriptures are full of errors and we can't take the Word of God literally, no real theological agreement can be reached.

We can be thankful for electronic media. Radio broadcasts in forty or fifty languages present the gospel. Too often, though, people hear the gospel but do not respond. Although television offers some good spiritual and religious programming, the modern TV industry promotes a reckless emphasis on entertainment and experience. Many media programs stress that they are looking for the real, the human Jesus. But, of course, He is more than human; He is the Son of God. Yet people are looking everywhere for Him except in the Scriptures.

The decline in the teaching of the Word of God is a serious concern. People are in the dark. Many pastors want to be intellectual and scholarly, but they fail to make the Bible clear. Many students are graduating today whose doctrinal position on many issues is unstable. They excuse themselves by saying that they want to be relevant and simply focus on the gospel. But if the pastors don't have an overall orientation to the entire message of Scripture, the gospel will slowly become confused and obscure in meaning.

Although the Bible and all that it teaches must be the central subject at a seminary, other subjects, too, fill out the overall understanding of spiritual issues. Dallas Theological Seminary was once questioned as to the curriculum being sufficiently broad to cover diverse theological perspectives. At that time I personally taught electives in Theology of Crisis, which covered the problems of Neo-orthodoxy and Barthianism, as well as courses dealing with modern and contemporary theologians and practically all liberal views. I also taught Theological Systems, which examined ancient, medieval, and modern theology, including the views of Augustine, Roman Catholic thought, Judaism, Unitarian doctrine, and Arminian theologies. In regard to methods, DTS doesn't attempt to follow the modernistic approach of overemphasis. We also offer studies in expository preaching, public speaking and reading, missionary principles and practices, religious education, and other courses. Of course, we were doing most of this within the basic four-year Th.M. program, which requires about 120 credit hours. Our distinction is plenty of hours in the biblical languages, theology, Bible exposition, and church history. A DTS graduate is indeed well trained.

I'm often asked what I think about posttribulational, midtribulational, or prewrath views on the Rapture. All of these positions in some way violate sound hermeneutics and contextual rules. I've found that most who advocate a position against a pretribulational Rapture do so for personal reasons rather than from scriptural interpretation. They say that the pretribulational view is too easy and that the church must be purged and sanctified by suffering through all or part of the Tribulation. Generally, such opponents interpret Matthew 24 as a Rapture passage: "Then there shall be two men in the field; one will be taken, and one will be left" (Matt. 24:40). This passage, however, is a record of what will happen at the Second Coming. Those taken are the unsaved, and they are purged out of the earth. The remaining are the saved, who will go into the millennial kingdom in their natural bodies to populate the millennial earth.

Views that are not pretribulational come and go. One advocate of an alternative position said, "In fifteen years everyone will be holding my view." I don't think that's happened, because hermeneutics and interpretation that are used to arrive at an understanding of these issues are based on solid principles. Many people who propose different views simply haven't thought them through. If one believes that prophecy is to be understood consistently and literally, one will not long hold to a wrong view.

Theological brushfires won't stop, however, until the Lord Jesus returns. After years of serving the Lord, I realize that doctrinal controversy will always raise its head. But, fortunately, strides toward orthodox doctrine do occur along the way. Take, for example, the Rapture novels, the "Left Behind" series, by Dr. Tim LaHaye and Jerry Jenkins. Through the publication of these books, millions of people are being exposed to the doctrine of the blessed hope. Although not everyone might agree with the fictional approach, thousands of people have come to Christ through reading the books in this series. Four and one-half years after it was initially published, the first book, *Left Behind,* was still selling at the rate of one hundred thousand copies per month. LaHaye has received thousands of letters from those who accepted Christ as their personal Savior. For every one person who wrote, it is estimated that ten more came to the Lord.

Around 1990, LaHaye shared my concern that studies on the issues of prophecy and the Rapture needed to be promoted. He called a meeting of thirty Bible scholars to a three-day meeting at a Dallas hotel. I attended, spoke, and added my support for starting a prophecy think-tank to reestablish interest in the blessed hope. All those in attendance noticed that the teaching of prophecy was waning around the country. From that humble beginning, the Pre-Trib Research Center was established. Hundreds of scholars and Bible teachers attend the yearly meetings. In the organization's first ten years, members produced hundreds of books on prophecy. Dr. LaHaye strongly believes that a resurgence of teaching the blessed hope has occurred, and he personally thanked me for my role in joining this group and helping him in that effort.

Although we moved closer to an apostate church in the 1990s, the Holy Spirit will still be at work right up until the Rapture. That might sound like a contradiction but, while each generation has its own form of apostasy, the Bible clearly states that things will get progressively worse: "The Spirit explicitly says that in later times some will fall away from the faith" (1 Tim. 4:1); "But realize this, that in the last days difficult times will come" (2 Tim. 3:1); "In the last days mockers will come with their mocking, following after their own lusts, and saying, 'Where is the promise of His coming?'" (2 Peter 3:3–4).

Could anything be more plain?

Changes are coming that will bring about a deepening and more ominous spiritual and moral darkness. But I intend to do what I can as a servant of the Lord. I enjoy teaching and preaching His Word, and I always give the gospel, no matter how much I think the audience knows about the Scriptures. And I will continue, as the old song says, *"to count [my] blessings, [and] name them one by one."*

12

IN MY FINAL YEARS

The decades that I served the Lord at DTS were blessed and fruitful. I was Dr. Lewis Chafer's assistant, I taught courses, helped edit books, and performed many administrative tasks. For sixteen years, from 1934 to 1950, I was pastor for Rosen Heights Presbyterian Church in Fort Worth. There, I tried to bless the congregation with the teaching of the Word of God, and those folks were certainly a blessing to Geraldine and me. When I became president of the seminary in 1952, the blessings continued as I taught the students who came our way. But I also had a lot of difficulties to overcome, adjusting to my role and struggling to get into a position from which I might properly lead the school.

When I began to make the writing of books a high priority, I felt good about what came off the presses. By publishing I was teaching many more than those in the classroom. Too, those books informed readers about Dallas Seminary, allowing people to read and study what the seminary was trying to communicate from the Scriptures. From the 1960s until my retirement as president, books were published, and enrollment increased, stimulating growth in teaching and administrative staff and the construction of buildings. Through those years, I watched the school struggle from its humble beginning to become a great institution with seventeen hundred students.

One of the delights of being involved in a seminary is the daily contact with students. It's a blessing to watch them stretch and grow spiritually and to see them go out into the field of service for Christ. That field is, of course, the world. We've seen graduates go forth as pastors, evangelists, missionaries, Bible school teachers, counselors, and media specialists. The list of occupations in which our graduates have served the body of Christ is long.

As the president did in the days when I was a student, I had to rein in a few pranksters. The administration had to put on a sober face with some of the students' antics, even when we were amused. A 1964 graduate, for example, told me of a student who, having worked late at night on the freight docks to make income, often sat at the back of the class, leaned his chair against the wall, and took a morning nap. On one occasion, the student sitting next to him jabbed him in the ribs and whispered, "The teacher has called on you to pray." The tired student leaped to his feet and began, "Our heavenly Father, we thank thee. . . ." The professor writing on the chalk board and the entire class thought that the poor fellow had completely lost his senses.

On another, not-so-funny, occasion, the students in Stearns Hall, the singles dorm, penciled a mustache on a very expensive portrait of Daniel Stearns that hung in the first floor lobby. The picture had been commissioned by the school's supportive Women's Auxiliary, who just happened to be arriving for one of their meetings in that room. At the morning chapel service, I announced that I would give the culprits just one hour to meet me in my office and confess their sin. They came; I spoke; they repented! It cost the school $250 to have the picture repaired. At the time, it wasn't funny, but now I can chuckle just a little. A blessing emerged from that mustache debacle, however. Some of those who pulled off the stunt ended up as Christian leaders.

My tenure with DTS, though fruitful and blessed, was even further enhanced by the presence of my wife. Geraldine admirably fulfilled the role of wife and mother. She excelled too as the wife of a seminary president, her warm Christian spirit spilling over into events at the school. No one has described Geraldine's faithful contribution better than did Mrs. John Witmer, wife of our librarian and one of our faculty members. Mrs. Witmer wrote in the spring 1986 seminary publication *Kindred Spirit,*

> In spite of ever increasing pressures on her time and talents, Geraldine continued to establish her priorities and, in the midst of it all, radiate an inner calm and assurance that showed the rewards of good stewardship and dependence on the Lord. Geraldine initiated many traditions at Dallas Seminary which continue to this day. Each year she hosted a faculty wives luncheon to introduce new faculty wives. Likewise, she organized monthly wives luncheons throughout the school year and presided at the times of prayer and business meetings that followed each luncheon.

In all of my ministry, Geraldine was a loving partner, who helped make possible whatever I have accomplished. In her ministry, she manifested multiple talents that seldom join in the same person, and which blossomed and matured over the years. She provided a loving basis for my ministry, without which it would have been much less effective. Our marriage itself was unusually congenial. Our son John, who is a licensed psychologist and family counselor, once observed that our marriage was one in a hundred because of our respect for one another and the evidence of our love.

In the pastorate at Rosen Heights, Geraldine was a new bride when she stepped in as pianist and a teacher of children. She led large classes on Wednesday and Sunday nights and provided leadership for women. When our pastorate terminated and we moved to Dallas, she taught Bible classes in our church and elsewhere. She taught the Scofield correspondence course to thirty-five seminary wives. Over three years, this course covers all major doctrines of the Bible and requires that the teacher possess a mastery of every book of the Bible. The experience gave Geraldine a basis from which she offered intelligent counsel to me in my own ministry.

When I became president of the seminary, Geraldine took over as advisor for the seminary wives before we had women students. The seminary's Wives Fellowship met on Thursday nights for two hours each week. A faculty member taught for one hour to help the wives understand the doctrine and theology that their husbands were receiving at seminary. The second hour was designed to provide training needed for effective ministry partnership with their husbands. The instruction covered almost every aspect of work a pastor's wife might perform in the church. Every six months, the wives elected a dozen or more officers, women who were usually untried and inexperienced. Geraldine counseled them and helped them learn to run an organization and plan a meeting. In her thirty years as advisor, Geraldine undoubtedly affected the lives and work of thousands of women.

Geraldine also directed the Women's Auxiliary of the seminary. That body met periodically during the year to support the seminary in various ways.

With all of her activities associated with the seminary and the church, Geraldine managed not only to maintain a household; she created a home. Interior decoration was Geraldine's special talent, but she also was a master in the kitchen, turning leftovers into an outstanding meal. It is difficult to find all of these abilities in one person, and it is understandable that I consider Geraldine the most wonderful woman in the world.

On the occasion of her retiring as advisor to wives, the seminary held a special program in her honor. They asked me to speak about my wife. I was hesitant about dealing with such a personal subject, but I presented three of Geraldine's outstanding characteristics that have meant the most to me. First, she never left any doubt as to her unconditional love for me. Second, her many talents in life and ministry were of great help to me. Third, she never criticized me in front of a third party.

Geraldine also has a wonderful sense of humor and a deep regard for her many friends. She has evinced a steadfast testimony in our life together, throughout both the heartaches and joy, and she will be long remembered by all who know her.

Sometimes wives are privy to things we men are not. Just before Mrs. Lewis Sperry Chafer died in 1944, she said to Geraldine, "We are training John to be the next president of Dallas Seminary." Eighteen years later, that bit of information shared in confidence became reality. And for thirty-four years my wife was "first lady" of DTS.

In addition to Geraldine's influence on my ministry at Dallas Seminary, John also had an important role. Shortly after graduating from seminary, he worked for a while in seminary promotion, at a time when we were facing the problem of rapidly growing enrollment and insufficient space. He came up with the idea of starting a capital fund for new buildings, something the seminary had never had before.

At first, I was dubious. But after several small meetings with donors and board members, it was determined that we should attempt this. However, the board turned down the idea of having a professional fund-raiser and put it more or less in my lap. In the end, we were able to raise the capital fund and build the Todd building as well as the Campbell building, two major educational buildings that were absolutely essential to any growth in enrollment. While we ended up taking a one-million-dollar loan from the bank, we were able to pay off the loan in just a few years.

At that time John also suggested that we have a capital fund drive for a student center. While the earlier fund for the academic buildings created quite a bit of enthusiasm and many pledges, people on the campus were slow to respond to the drive. However, in an amazingly short time many responses to mail appeals for gifts were received to justify beginning the building. We were able to secure a two-million-dollar line of credit from the bank and arranged to pay the contractor actual construction costs each month as they arose. The money kept coming in, and each month we were able to pay the contractor without borrowing. Eventually the entire building was completed, paid for with over three million dollars raised. It was an amazing evidence of the Lord's sufficiency, as most of the gifts were in response to fundraising letters. Today we would not know what to do without the student center.

The time finally came when it seemed right to relinquish my position as president of DTS. I had previously told the chairman of the board at the time, William Seay, that I wanted to retire when I had served the seminary for fifty years. That's what I did. On April 1, 1986, after serving the school for fifty years, I retired. I didn't have any doubts about doing it. Some people think they have to retire at age sixty, and they quit too soon. I retired at age seventy-five, but I did more after I was sixty than I did in all of the years before.

In March 1988, at the age of seventy-eight, and just two years after stepping up to the position of chancellor, I had a heart attack. I got to the hospital quickly, but in the intensive care ward I had another attack. The doctors thought that another episode would kill me, but somehow I knew that the Lord would not be taking me home just yet. That evening, I underwent a quadruple bypass. The danger wasn't over; while recovering I contracted a staph infection. Although recovery was slow, taking a full year, I didn't became discouraged or think that the Lord was putting me out to pasture.

Then in September 1994 I broke a hip, which required years for recovery. I believe in the providence of God, that those two physical bumps in the road were under God's sovereignty: "Even though I walk through the valley of the shadow of death, I fear no evil; for Thou art with me" (Ps. 23:4); "Bless the LORD, O my soul, and forget none of His benefits" (Ps. 103:2); "[He] heals all your diseases" (v. 3).

I've been blessed most of my life with good health and physical strength, and I wanted my energy and vitality to return. I wanted to travel to churches, and preach and teach the Scriptures again. But both physical setbacks confined me to a bed and a chair. For many people my age, two such serious problems would suppress productivity and even the will to stay alive. But God had more tasks for me to do.

It seems that in my old age I've become a curiosity. My Bible conference ministry across the country originally began in the early 1940s as a substitute for Dr. Chafer or Dr. Ironside when illness prevented either of them from fulfilling an engagement.

As time went on, I received an increasing number of speaking invitations, resulting in several Bible conference appearances each month throughout the United States and Canada, and in South America, Central America, Australia, New Zealand, Europe, and the Middle East. Alongside the conference ministry developed a widespread book ministry. With more than 4 million in print, doors opened to many places because people wanted to hear the author.

Since 1994, I've continued to travel about the country preaching. At ninety, I'm a voice out of the past, and somehow this gives credence to what I teach. I've become the grandpa that many people want to see and hear. Maybe in these late years I've more to say, or perhaps I'm simply reiterating what I've always taught about the imminent coming of Christ. But for some reason, it just sounds better from a Bible teacher my age.

I want to be remembered as a person who was faithful to the Word of God, one who never changed or weakened his conviction. When people get older they sometimes become more strict or too liberal in their views. Not only has my personality remained the same but my attitudes about the things of God have not changed. Frankly, I don't think much about how I'm to be remembered. Although I will be remembered, that is not my goal. As I began my ministry, I struggled to do what God wanted me to, whether it was leading a small church or teaching at the seminary. It never occurred to me to build monuments or to be a great leader. However God chooses to use us is His business. The apostle Paul wrote, "Not that we are adequate in ourselves to consider anything as coming from ourselves, but our adequacy is from God, who also made us adequate as servants of a new covenant" (2 Cor. 3:5–6).

So I don't care what people say, good or bad. As far as I

know, I've done the will of God, and I'm satisfied with that. I learned to let go of criticism and not pay much attention to those who simply want to argue. Even after turning ninety, I still receive hate mail for some of the things I teach about prophecy or other doctrines of Scripture. Some people have castigated me for teaching the Rapture of the church and even the eternal security of the believer.

But there's another side of the coin. When I turned ninety, I received more than nine hundred complimentary letters that filled two huge albums. The school gave me a birthday party at which speakers praised all that I had done. Each speaker tried to outdo the one before. They all meant well, of course. But I sat there wondering, *Who are they talking about?*

In my final years, if the Rapture doesn't occur before I die, I want to go out teaching His Word. No verse better puts my life in proper perspective than Philippians 1:21: "For to me, to live is Christ, and to die is gain."

13

CHRONOLOGY OF THE LIFE OF
JOHN F. WALVOORD

May 1, 1910	Born in Sheboygan, Wisconsin	1910	British suffragettes adopt violent tactics in voting rights campaign
September 1925	Trusts Jesus as Savior	1925	Al Capone takes over Chicago South Side gang
January 1928	High school graduation; matriculation at Wheaton	1928	U.S. women over 21 given right to vote
June 1929	First missionary work in Nebraska	1929	First Arab–Jew clash in Palestine; October Stock Market crash
June 1931	B.A. degree from Wheaton College	1931	First disease preventing vaccines widely available
September 1931	Student at Dallas Seminary		
January 1932	Meets Geraldine Lundgren	1932	U.S. unemployment tops 12 million in Depression
November 1932	John G. Walvoord, father, dies at age 60		
May 1934	Receives Th.B., Th.M. degrees from DTS	1934	German President Hindenburg dies; Adolf Hitler becomes führer
September 1934	Pastor, Rosen Heights Presbyterian Church, Fort Worth, Texas		
September 1935	Temporary registrar, DTS	1935	Jewish persecution begins in Germany with Nuremberg Laws

April 1936	Registrar, DTS	1936	German troops break
May 1936	Receives Th.D. from DTS		Treaty of Versailles by
			occupying the Rhineland;
September 1936	Teaches half of DTS		Heinrich Focke flies first
	theology courses		helicopter; Hoover Dam
			opens
June 1939	Marries Geraldine	1939	German invasion of
			Poland begins World
			War II on September 1
February 1942	Son, John, born	1942	Japanese capture Manila
September 1942	Work begins on M.A. at		and Singapore
	Texas Christian		
1943	*The Holy Spirit* published	1943	U.S. attacks Japanese-
			held islands
February 1945	Son, James, born	1945	Germany surrenders May
Spring 1945	Dr. Chafer suffers stroke		8; Japan surrenders
August 1945	M.A. degree from Texas		August 15
	Christian		
September 1945	Becomes Dr. Chafer's		
	assistant		
1947–48	Chafer, *Systematic*	1947	United Nations parti-
	Theology publishing		tions Palestine into Arab
	project		and Jewish states; Arabs
			reject proposal
		1948	David Ben-Gurion
			proclaims establishment
			of Israel on May 14;
			Arabs attack Jewish
			settlements
Fall 1950	Pastorate ends at Rosen	1950	North Korea invades
	Heights Church		South Korea
August 1952	Death of Dr. Chafer	1952	Elizabeth II of England
October 1952	Appointment to DTS		crowned
	presidency		
February 1953	Installation as president	1953	Dwight D. Eisenhower
	of DTS		becomes U.S. president;
			Korean War ends

April 1954	Son, Timothy, born	1954	Roger Bannister runs mile in under four minutes
1955	*The Thessalonian Letters, The Return of the Lord* published	1955	Tension builds on Israel–Jordan border
1957	Son, Paul, born *The Rapture Question, Inspiration and Interpretation,* published	1957	Russia launches first space satellite, Sputnik 1
1959	*The Millennial Kingdom* published	1959	Hawaii fiftieth U.S. state
1961	First trip to Middle East *To Live Is Christ, Philippians* published	1961	Berlin Wall erected
1962	*Israel in Prophecy* published	1962	Cuban missile crisis takes U.S. and Russia to brink of nuclear war
1963	*Truth for Today,* Biblotheca Sacra *Reader* (coeditor)		
1964	*The Church in Prophecy* published	1964	Race riots in U.S. cities
1966	*The Revelation of Jesus Christ* published	1966	Vietnam War protests divide U.S.
1967	*The Nations in Prophecy* published	1967	Six-Day War between Arab states and Israel; Israeli victory expands national territory
1969	*Jesus Christ Our Lord* published; authority increases at DTS	1969	U.S. begins withdrawal of troops from South Vietnam
1971	*Daniel* published	1971	Soviet spacecraft lands on Mars
1973	*The Holy Spirit at Work Today* published	1973	Yom Kippur War in Middle East; world oil crisis follows

1974	*Armageddon, Oil and the Middle East* published	1974	U.S. President Nixon resigns over Watergate scandal
	Matthew: Thy Kingdom Come published		
	Chafer's *Major Bible Themes*, revised		
November 1974	Mary Walvoord, mother, dies at age 101		
1976	*The Blessed Hope and the Tribulation* published		
1977	*Philippians: Triumph in Christ* published		
June 1979	Son Timothy killed in car accident after completing medical school	1979	Israel and Egypt sign territorial peace treaty
1983	Bibliotheca Sacra *Reader* (coeditor)		
1983–1985	*The Bible Knowledge Commentary* set published (coeditor)	1985	World population reaches 4.5 billion
April 1986	Steps down as president; named DTS chancellor	1986	U.S. space shuttle *Challenger* explodes on takeoff, killing crew of seven
1988	*The Nations, Israel and the Church in Prophecy* published in one volume	1988	Bloody, decade-long Iran–Iraq War ends
1988	*Systematic Theology* by Lewis Sperry Chafer abridged		
March 1988	Heart attack, bypass surgery		
1989	*The Life of Christ Commentary* (coeditor)		
1990	*What We Believe* published; *The Prophecy Knowledge Handbook* (later retitled *Every Prophecy of the Bible*) published	1990	Iraq invasion of Kuwait triggers Gulf War

1991	*Armageddon* (rev.), *Major Bible Prophecies* published	1991	U.N. forces Iraq to withdraw from Kuwait; war ends
July 1994	Brother-in-law and colleague Ellwood Evans dies		
September 1994	Hip shattered; repaired through surgery		
1997	*The Final Drama* (formerly *Prophecy*) published		
1998	*End Times* published		
January 1998	Sister-in-law Harriet Evans dies		
2001	*Prophecy in the New Millennium* published	2001	George W. Bush sworn in as U.S. President
May 2001	Made chancellor emeritus, DTS		

14

SELECTED LETTERS FROM WELL-WISHERS ON DR. WALVOORD'S NINETIETH BIRTHDAY, MAY 1, 2000

Barbara and I want to add our personal greetings to those of your family and friends as you celebrate your ninetieth birthday. Congratulations. . . . God bless you as you continue His work at Dallas Theological Seminary.

—George Bush
Former President of the United States

I appreciate your work as a scholar, author, and theologian of distinction and your service as Chancellor of Dallas Theological Seminary. . . . Laura joins me in sending best wishes for a wonderful birthday celebration.

—George W. Bush
Governor of Texas
(Current President of the United States)

Thank you, my friend, for modeling the life of Christ so consistently and so faithfully through the years. . . . We rejoice with you over God's grace and goodness. May He reward you abundantly!

—Dr. Charles Swindoll
President
Dallas Theological Seminary

I am grateful for your considerable influence on my life and ministry—as my teacher and advisor during my student years; as my mentor and example of skilled leadership during my years of "apprenticeship"; and as a continuing friend and supporter during my years as president.

—Dr. Don Campbell
President Emeritus
Dallas Theological Seminary

No one in your lifetime has done as much as you have to clarify and proclaim the blessed truth of His coming. You are God's great gift to the Body [of Christ].

—Dr. J. Dwight Pentecost
Distinguished Professor Emeritus
Dallas Theological Seminary

Thanks for the great influence you have been to us. We thank God for you and for the way He uses you for His glory.

—Dr. Ronald Blue
President of Central American Mission

History bears witness that those who begin well often end poorly. Exceptions to this rule, therefore, stand out as giants worthy of admiration, emulation, and praise. You are one of those servants of Christ, Dr. Walvoord, who have inspired us to go beyond what we thought we could be and do.

—Dr. Eugene Merrill
Professor of Old Testament
Dallas Theological Seminary

Thank you for your faithfulness to the Word of God, to sound doctrine, to Geraldine and your family, to responsible evangelical witness, to the teaching of your students (who must number in the many thousands) and your love of all the saints. . . . With highest respect and love.

—Dr. Edward L. Hayes
President Emeritus
Denver Seminary

I am grateful for our many years of friendship, starting with my enrollment at DTS in 1952 when you assumed leadership of the Seminary. I am also grateful for my time as a member of the Board of Regents and later as your Executive Assistant during those historic days in the expansion of the Seminary.

—Steven E. Slocum
Class of '56
Dallas Theological Seminary

Your classes, Dr. Chafer's classes, and the classes especially of Dr. S. Lewis Johnson have been a tremendous blessing, and I have sought to be a faithful steward in investing these things in the lives of many of God's servants who have served Him in Latin America, Spain, and the islands of the Caribbean where Spanish is spoken. I am grateful for your impact on my life when we went to the island of Dominica and served there from 1953 to 1955.

—Dr. George G. Parker
Instructor, Rio Grande Bible Institute

We thank God for you and for your leadership at Dallas Seminary down through the years. And we have fond memories of our years of college and seminary together. Especially playing tag in the YMCA swimming pool in Dallas.

—Dr. Willard M. Aldrich
President Emeritus
Multnomah School of Bible

I came to Dallas Seminary after graduating from Multnomah, feeling I wasn't ready to be a pastor. After about two years I became discouraged, thinking I was repeating much of what I had learned previously. I visited with you and said I was leaving and wanted to begin to minister. You reminded me I had promised to complete four years of training; I stayed, graduated, and how I thank you for keeping me on track!

—Oscar Hegg
Class of '46
Dallas Theological Seminary

You having become president of DTS the year I entered, as well as your graduating from Horlick High School in Racine, and your attending Union Tabernacle, now Racine Bible Church, has caused my wife Lois and me to feel very close to you and your dear wife, Geraldine, over these many years. I felt favored by our Lord to have had you as my Theology Professor and also to speak in the church at Racine. Your impact on my life and ministry continues to bear fruit and

I will always hold you in high esteem because the Lord is so much at home in your life and labors for Him.

—Philip L. Whisenhunt
Class of '56
Dallas Theological Seminary

Thank you for the significant impact you've had in my life, from sitting under your ministry, learning to put prophetic truth together, hearing your evangelistic passion. You've modeled Christlike love along with a commitment to the truth. I trust God will continue to bless the many seeds you've planted and watered for His glory.

—Don Hawkins
Producer
Back to the Bible

When our freshman class was invited to your home for an "ice cream sundae" get-acquainted social, I was more than a little nervous. You stood by the gallon containers of ice cream and scooped out generous helpings to us as we came by. In the process of covering my abundant supply of ice cream, I nervously dripped chocolate sauce on my shirt and tie. What happened next had a lot to do with my being able to adjust to the wonderful rigorous program that first year. You loaned me a fresh shirt and immediately cleaned my tie—your wife Geraldine took my stained shirt and washed it and gave it back to me before we left that evening. The mature and dignified example of your leadership of the seminary and the wonderful theological teaching we received from you in your Christology class could never surpass the example of Christ living in you that evening when you ministered to a very uncomfortable young student in a gracious, kind, and very personal way. I hope to have the privilege of visiting with you on your 100th birthday celebration!

—Art Robertson
Senior Pastor
Ridgeway Alliance Church

Thank you for the many ways you have helped me personally. In 1950, you allowed me to enter your upper division course on Contemporary Theology when I was only an undergraduate student. In 1958 and again in 1973 you opened positions for me in the theology department. In 1996 you graciously wrote the forward to my book *Witnesses in Stone* published by Kregel. Your steadfast and unswerving loyalty to our Lord and to the Word of God are a singular blessing to your wide circle of friends and loved ones.

—Frederic R. Howe
Professor Emeritus
Dallas Theological Seminary

Your counsel and our preparation for seeking and obtaining our Commission for the Army Chaplaincy was greatly appreciated. My wife Jean and I pray that the Lord will allow further years of ministry and encouragement to those who desire to maintain the historic stance of DTS in these troublesome days.

—Raymond A. Acker
Chaplain (LTC) USA, Retired

I was a student at DTS 1958–62. I remember our studies with you in Christology, pneumatology, and eschatology. . . . One of the struggles concerned the pre-trib Rapture position. You asked me to come visit. That office visit was the beginning of helping me clearly think through the position. You asked two basic questions: 1) "Do you believe there is a future time of tribulation?" My response was, "Yes." 2) "Do you believe that Christ could come at any minute?" My response was, "Yes." You said, "Then you believe in the pre-trib Rapture." I have become more convinced and confirmed in this position as the years have passed. Thanks so much for your good help and patience with the likes of me.

—Cary M. Perdue
Senior Pastor
Sugar Grove Church, Goshen, Indiana

Dr. Walvoord, several incidents stand out to me as a student. The Spiritual Life Class was a rich time of blessing, made so by your humble and godly spirit as you taught the class. Also, you graciously spoke at one of our early-morning class breakfasts. I don't remember your message that morning, but was impressed that you had taken time to have your devotions that morning in spite of the very early hour. Also, I was impacted by your incredible grasp of prophetic Scripture, which gave me a love for the truth concerning the imminent return of Christ. . . . What stands out to me above all else is your godly character and humble spirit.

—Allan M. Stensvad
Pastor, First Baptist Church
Philomath, Oregon

I thank my God upon every remembrance of you—Philippians 1:3. I am thankful for your clear, uncomplicated communication of Scripture and its doctrinal content. I appreciate this more every year as I associate with leaders in

Evangelicalism who do not know or understand what the Bible teaches. . . . It is a privilege to thank you, to pay tribute to you, and to extend my best wishes to you on this milestone occasion. And my best wishes to Mrs. Walvoord, who stood by you and helped make it all happen.

—Dr. Howard F. Vos
Professor of History and Archaeology Emeritus
The King's College

Thirteen years ago you were up in the New York metropolitan area doing a prophecy conference. My wife Sarah and I just had our fourth child and there was some concern at the time about her health. I mentioned this to you at a dinner that was given for area pastors and you said that you would share this with your wife and pray about it. I knew how busy a man you were so I never expected to hear back from you concerning Marcy's health. A week or two later, however, a letter came from you asking about Marcy. That was indeed special that you would have cared enough to write such a letter! Today I am still enjoying the rich benefits of being a student and a graduate of DTS.

—Jeff Gowesky
Pastor, Goshen Baptist Church
West Chester, Pennsylvania

As a sophomore student at DTS I took the course on prophecy with you that was required of all students. I remember how impressed I was with your textbook *The Millennial Kingdom* used in the class. I was also fear-struck by you because you appeared so sober and business-like. Looking back, I now understand that you were terribly busy with so many responsibilities. But as the years have rolled by I now see things in a different light. I have come to learn that you are one of the warmest and most sincere ministers of the Lord Jesus I've ever met. Now, in my own final years of ministry, I've been given one of the greatest privileges any DTS graduate could have, namely, helping to write the biography of your theological journey. In my interviewing time with you, you made two statements I'll never ever forget. During one of our discussions about the return of the Lord, glancing out the window and with warm feelings and a faraway but hopeful look, you said, "Maybe today is the day He'll come back!" On another occasion when we were talking about the problems people have in this life, you remarked, "I don't judge people; I leave that to the Lord. And after all, we're all just sinners!" These and other simple but profound utterances came from the depths of your heart. Thank you for sharing from your soul such intimate thoughts about spiritual and eternal matters.

—Mal Couch
President, Tyndale Theological Seminary
Fort Worth, Texas

RESOURCES

Further helpful reference material on the life of John F. Walvoord:

Campbell, Donald K. *Walvoord: A Tribute.* Chicago: Moody, 1982.

Mink, Timothy G. "John F. Walvoord at Dallas Theological Seminary." Doctoral dissertation, North Texas State University, 1987.

Walvoord, John F. Papers of John F. Walvoord. Archives, Dallas Theological Seminary.

BOOKS BY DR. JOHN F. WALVOORD

	Title	Publisher	Date
contributor	*Modem Debating*	Follett	1932
contributor	*Not by Bread Alone*	Zondervan	1940
contributor	*The Sure Word of Prophecy*	Revell	1942
contributor	*Winona Echoes*	Zondervan	1943
author	*The Doctrine of the Holy Spirit*	Dallas Seminary	1943
contributor	*Light for the World's Darkness*	Loizeaux	1944
author	*The Holy Spirit*	Zondervan	1954
author	*The Return of the Lord*	Zondervan	1955
author	*The Thessalonian Epistles*	Zondervan	1956
contributor	*Understanding the Times*	Zondervan	1956
author	*The Rapture Question*	Zondervan	1957, rev. & enl. 1979
editor	*Inspiration and Interpretation*	Eerdmans	1957
author	*The Millennial Kingdom*	Zondervan	1959
contributor	*The Word for This Century*	Oxford University	1960
author	*To Live Is Christ*	Dunham	1961
coauthor	*The Prophetic Word in Crisis Days*	Dunham	1961
author	*Israel in Prophecy*	Zondervan	1962
editor	*Truth for Today: Bibliotheca Sacra Reader*	Moody	1963

contributor	*The Coming World Church*	Back to the Bible	1963
author	*The Church in Prophecy*	Zondervan	1964
contributor	*Focus on Prophecy*	Revell	1964
author	*The Revelation of Jesus Christ*	Moody	1966
author	*The Nations in Prophecy*	Zondervan	1967
contributor	*Fresh Winds of the Holy Spirit*	Bethel College & Seminary	1968
contributor	*Prophetic Truth Unfolding Today*	Revell	1968
author	*Jesus Christ Our Lord*	Moody	1969
author	*Daniel: The Key to Prophetic Revelation*	Moody	1971
author	*Philippians: Triumph in Christ*	Moody	1971
contributor	*Prophecy in the Making*	Creation House	1971
contributor	*Prophecy and the Seventies*	Moody	1971
author	*The Holy Spirit at Work Today*	Moody	1973
editor	*Major Bible Themes* (Revised)	Zondervan	1974
coauthor	*Armageddon, Oil and the Middle East Crisis*	Zondervan	1974, rev. & enl. 1990
author	*Matthew: Thy Kingdom Come*	Kregel	1974, rep. 1998
contributor	*Jesus the King Is Coming*	Moody	1975
contributor	*Founder's Week Messages*	Moody	1975
author	*The Blessed Hope and the Tribulation*	Zondervan	1976
contributor	*America in History and Bible Prophecy*	Moody	1976
coeditor	*The Bib Sac Reader*	Moody	1983
coeditor	*Bible Knowledge Commentary*, 2 vols.	Victor	1983, 1985
coauthor	*Five Views on Sanctification*	Zondervan	1987
editor	*Chafer's Systematic Theology Abridged*	Victor	1988
author	*The Nations, Israel, and the Church in Prophecy*	Zondervan	1988

coeditor	*The Life of Christ Commentary*	Victor	1989
contributor	*Money for Ministries*	Victor	1989
author	*Every Prophecy of the Bible* (formerly *The Prophecy Knowledge Handbook*)	Victor	1990
author	*What We Believe*	Discovery House	1990
author	*Major Bible Prophecies*	Zondervan	1991
coauthor	*Four Views on Hell*	Zondervan	1992
author	*The Final Drama* (formerly *Prophecy*)	Kregel	1993, rep. 1997
contributor	*Issues in Dispensationalism*	Moody	1994
contributor	*Vital Theological Issues*	Kregel	1994
contributor	*Vital Prophetic Issues*	Kregel	1995
contributor	*Raging into Apocalypse*	New Leaf	1995
contributor	*Foreshocks of Antichrist*	Harvest House	1997
contributor	*Vital Christology Issues*	Kregel	1997
author	*End Times*	Word	1998
contributor	*Forewarning*	Harvest House	1998
contributor	*The Road to Armageddon*	Word	1999
contributor	*Countdown to Armageddon*	Harvest House	1999
contributor	*Foreshadows of Wrath and Redemption*	Harvest House	1999
author	*Prophecy in the New Millennium*	Kregel	2001